Liberty

A PATH TO ITS RECOVERY

BY F. A. HARPER

THE FOUNDATION FOR ECONOMIC EDUCATION

IRVINGTON-ON-HUDSON, NEW YORK · 1949

Published by The Foundation for Economic Education; FEE.org.

Large Print Edition published 2012 by Skyler J. Collins.
Visit: www.skylerjcollins.com

Cover image by StockFreeImages.com.

ISBN-13: 978-1480032460
ISBN-10: 1480032468

EDITOR'S NOTE

Dr. Floyd A. Harper has been a member of the staff of The Foundation for Economic Education since 1946. He came to The Foundation from Cornell University, where he had served as Professor of Marketing for over a decade.

His writings, which are characterized by down-to-earth practicality, include numerous articles and booklets, and the notable books *The World's Hunger* (with F. A. Pearson) and *The Crisis of the Free Market.*

Dr. Harper's occupation is economics; his preoccupation is liberty. His thinking is here offered as a stimulant to independent thinking, and as an antidote to collective apathy.

ABOUT THIS EXPLORATION

MINDFUL OF THE SCOPE and complexity of the problem of liberty, these exploratory remarks on the subject are offered with humility as a progress report. It is hoped that they may stimulate further thought and study of this most important problem, among those who will disagree as well as among those who will agree.

Present associates and others deserve credit for the inspiration that has resulted in the development of these concepts of liberty. Probably most of the ideas have been contributed by them, though the origin of any idea cannot be traced. The parts that meet with their disapproval, however, are solely the responsibility of the author; he has not been asked to bend a word or a phrase against his own judgment, in deference to the differing opinions of any other persons.

Though these are the author's beliefs at the time of writing, he expects and welcomes honest disagreement. His own opinion will undoubtedly change on certain points as a result of evidence or reasoning not now at his command.

The path to truth is always strewn with the wreckage of ideas once held and later discarded, either by the person who held them or by others. Differing opinions and changes of opinion are the rights of persons under the subject being discussed — *Liberty*.

F. A. HARPER

May, 1949

CONTENTS

PART ONE: THE DESIGN OF LIBERTY

PART TWO: ON MEASURING LIBERTY

PART THREE: THE PRESENT PROBLEM

APPENDICES

PART 1

THE DESIGN OF LIBERTY

The world has never had a good definition of the word liberty, and the American people, just now, are much in want of one. We all declare for liberty, but in using the same word we do not all mean the same thing. With some the word liberty may mean for each man to do as he pleases with himself, and the product of his labor; while with others the same word may mean for some men to do as they please with other men, and the product of other men's labor. Here are two, not only different but incompatible things, called by the same name — liberty. And it follows that each of the things is, by the respective parties, called by two different and incompatible names — liberty and tyranny.

ABRAHAM LINCOLN

CHAPTER ONE

THE NATURE OF LIBERTY

Opinions differ widely about liberty. They differ widely as to what comprises liberty, as to how much of it we now enjoy, as to the amount that has been lost in this country.

The extent of difference of opinion as to what comprises liberty is indicated by the widely differing ideologies whose advocates claim to be correct in their particular concept of liberty. This includes the Republicans, Democrats, Socialists and all the other political organizations. It includes most civilian organizations of various sorts, such as the churches. It includes the United States, Britain and Russia. All claim to be championing the cause of liberty.

Many persons are unconcerned about liberty, which is still another attitude toward it. Many seem to consider liberty to be a thing of geography or of heredity. These persons loll in unconcern because they feel assured that liberty is safe in this country to which their ancestors once fled from autocratic tyrannies abroad. They seem to be unaware that the sons of free men may become slaves even in a land where a high degree of liberty has reigned.

Whatever the reasons for these widely differing beliefs about liberty, it is certain that harmony of action requires, as the first step, agreement on what comprises liberty; otherwise it is impossible to agree on its presence or absence, or on the conditions now suppressing liberty.

The main purpose of this study is to offer a concept of liberty that may serve as a guide to its recovery. First I will give my concept of the nature of liberty and of the function of government in maintaining a liberal society.[1]

The spirit of liberty, denuded of philosophical terms, was expressed thus by a child of eleven years:

> I'm nobody but myself,
> And myself is only me.
> I'm only myself in doings and ways,
> And my mind is mine only, you see.

This verse reflects on the fact that liberty is an individual matter; that without liberty for the individual, there is no liberty at all. To recognize the individual nature of liberty is not to deny, as will be discussed later, that it is possible for "government" or other agencies to serve in defense of liberty. But first there is need to survey the individual nature of liberty so that it will not be lost from sight in a discussion of "group action"—government, democracy, organization.

Liberty exists when a person is free to do whatever he desires, according to his wisdom and conscience.

This definition of liberty may well prove shocking. There may be an immediate temptation to say: "Yes, but . . . ," and to consider it no further. But such a reaction may merely suggest how far we have strayed from an understanding of liberty, and from the intelligent devotion that is necessary for day-by-day decisions that would assure liberty. If that be our plight, and if liberty is to prevail, there must be a willingness to open one's mind to a discussion of the subject that may run head-on into some previously

[1] The analysis is founded on certain hypotheses in the form of faiths. These are discussed in Appendix I, "Faiths About the Nature and Destiny of Man."

accepted beliefs. Unfortunately, it is impossible to discuss every aspect of this complex problem first, in order to relieve the shock; some choice of sequence in treating parts of the problem is necessary.

A HERMIT IS UNCONCERNED about liberty. To him it is not a problem so long as he remains a hermit. His problem, as a free person, is to live with himself and with his God. He is free to do as he wishes within the confines of his wisdom and conscience — a limitation not considered to be a restriction of liberty, as that term is used herein.

Liberty becomes a matter of concern only when there arises the danger of losing it, or after it has been lost. Loss of liberty is possible only because of the things persons do to each other. The problem of liberty is, then, exclusively in the realm of relationships between persons.

The hermit, who lacks contact with all other persons, enjoys liberty to the full; it is no problem to him. But should he join "society," and come to have relationships with others, liberty would then become a problem to him because its loss would then have become a threat. Others might then infringe upon his liberty; as an extreme, they might make him their slave.

As a problem of our concern, liberty has to do with all those things that comprise "society," and nothing else. This includes all purchases and sales; it includes arrangements whereby some persons work for others; it includes voting for President, listening to the school teacher or to the preacher, and all other similar events common to everyday life. These are the areas where liberty is at stake. These are the realms in which one person may rob another of his liberty, and thus prevent him from doing whatever he wishes according to his wisdom and conscience.

Liberty is often termed an "inalienable right." It is inalienable (incapable of being surrendered or lost) only to a hermit while he remains a hermit. For all who live in society, liberty is alienable and may be lost. And that is precisely the reason for concern about it.

Although liberty is under threat in all human relationships, it need not be surrendered because of these relationships. Liberty need not be lost, as is frequently asserted, in proportion as these relationships are increased. In fact, the preservation of liberty is a requisite to continued social development and to an advancing civilization.

A relationship between persons must be either voluntary or involuntary. Liberty remains inviolate in any voluntary relationship because, being voluntary, the act is in accordance with the wishes of the participants — which is liberty. Thus it is only the involuntary relationships wherein liberty is violated.

The nature of voluntary relationships can be illustrated by two men who agree to exchange labor in the building of their houses. The exchange is arranged because of the mutual advantage that is expected. One of them may be the better carpenter and the other the better mason. They can build their houses quicker and better by each working at his specialty on both houses. This is the principle of "division of labor," by which civilization has been able to advance and the level of living to be raised. Each person concentrates on his specialty, and trades any excess over his own wants for the excesses of other things offered by other specialists — all voluntarily exchanged in free markets. It is the same principle that makes possible a symphony instead of solos.

If one makes another person his slave and compels him to labor on his house, it is an involuntary act; the liberty of the person enslaved has been violated.

All voluntary relationships rest on the principle of cooperation, either consciously or unconsciously. They rest on the spirit of cooperation, that is, rather than on any special form of "cooperation" as defined in some law. The cooperative feature is evidenced by the fact that both sides of a deal enter into it willingly, because each of them expects it to be to his advantage. Each side, to be sure, enters the deal because of a selfish interest; he enters it for his own personal gain. But the same motive applies to the other side too. By viewing both sides, the cooperative aspect of mutual advantage is revealed in every instance of a voluntary human relationship. Lacking the prospect of mutual advantage, the event would not have occurred voluntarily.

It is not necessary, therefore, that liberty be lost as society becomes more and more involved. Such an assertion, by the devout hermit or by one bent on the destruction of liberty, is in error. The development of society does, however, involve a threat to liberty. And any developing society which ignores the threat and fails to meet it, or which falls victim to the fatalistic view that a loss of liberty is inevitable under advancing civilization, will itself fail and fall.

CHAPTER TWO

FORMS OF LIBERTY

IN SPEAKING OF LIBERTY, relationships between persons are sometimes classified into types.

One such attempt was the listing of the "four freedoms" — freedom of speech, of worship, from want and from fear — which seems deficient since all these freedoms are enjoyed by an inmate of a federal penitentiary. Anyone who considers these freedoms to be complete in their coverage, and who is distressed because he does not now enjoy full freedom, can easily acquire "freedom" for the rest of his life by committing a crime leading to a life sentence in a penitentiary.

There have been other attempts to list the types of liberty. There could be any number of listings, because any classification must of necessity be arbitrary.

It may be useful, however, to consider three distinct areas of liberty:

1. Beliefs — thoughts, ideas, faiths
2. Physical relationships
3. Economic affairs

The nature of the first and second — beliefs and actions — includes such commonplace items as one's belief about the shape of the earth or the existence of a Deity, and the association of courtship or of a fishing trip.

Economic affairs are those of production, exchange and use of goods and services, which are involved in human activity because they are both desired and scarce enough not to be free — potatoes, houses, opera and all the others.

Confusion among the three areas of liberty may result from their being joined, as they commonly are in daily affairs. All three are involved, for instance, when two workmen discuss religion while operating at the ends of a crosscut saw, or when a man pays alimony for having beaten his wife after she had expressed her opinion of him.

The three aspects will be discussed separately, or unscrambled, as an aid to understanding the elements of the problem of liberty.

A BELIEF is a purely personal matter, always inalienable so far as liberty is concerned. It is not a thing exposed in the same manner as a physical act or an economic act. One person cannot hold a belief for another, as he can hold the other's hand or his horse. Nor can a belief be bought and sold like wheat.

Such a concept of beliefs may be difficult to grasp, because beliefs are commonly confused with the overt evidences of belief. The distinction is important, however, in gaining a clear concept of the problem of liberty as it relates to matters of beliefs, such as thoughts, ideas and faiths.

A belief is only in a person's mind. He may choose to reveal his belief to others, by speaking it or writing it. When he does so, the thing revealed is an overt expression of belief instead of being the belief itself. One may, in fact, proclaim a belief that is the direct opposite of the belief he truly holds, if he wishes to mislead his listener.

The difference between a belief and the expression of a belief may be illustrated by events in the life of Columbus. He believed the earth to be round, but that belief was independent of its being either expressed to anyone or indicated by any action. He expressed the belief to Queen Isabella in the hope of gaining financial help for his expedition to the Indies, and also by the act of setting sail. He might have falsified his belief, to avoid scorn or persecution, by declaring that he believed the earth to be flat while continuing to believe it to be round.

Communism offers another illustration. It is said to embrace falsehood as a proper weapon for purposes of concealment and defense. Laws and regulations aimed at it by its enemies must depend solely on evidences of belief that fall within the area of possible falsehood. How can a sincere denial of membership in the communist party or of devotion to that cause, be distinguished from a false one?

Expressions of belief are worth no more than the integrity of the person, and integrity is not to be judged by mere expressions of one's belief or by any claims of integrity. The best evidence of belief is the nature of one's action. When Columbus set sail, he was offering worthy evidence of his actual beliefs. When a person opposes measures which give vehicle to the points in the Communist Manifesto, that is worthy evidence of his beliefs.

Liberty is not in danger so far as a person's belief is concerned, because in this respect he is of necessity a hermit and unavoidably free. He is at liberty to continue to believe as he will, in spite of all the dictators in the world and in spite of all the power they can grasp. The dictator may take a person's land, his cattle, his family, his life; but he can never grab a person's belief, because it lacks a handle for grabbing.

It is the expressions of belief, not the beliefs themselves, that are threatened with loss of liberty. The danger is in connection with those devices by which one reveals his beliefs to others, such as printing and distributing evidences of them through the mails, using the radio, or meeting with others in a church for purposes of overt expressions of religious belief. These are the things attacked by those who would destroy liberty.

Tools for the expression of beliefs are mainly economic matters. If they are not directly economic matters, they at least employ economic devices for carrying out the exchange of information or for the demonstration of beliefs. The newspaper or the radio, or some land and a building where a meeting is to be held, all involve physical acts or economic considerations. The problem of liberty arises only in these spheres.

"Thought control" is then an impossibility, in any direct sense, because thought is a personal process with no handle for direct control. Possibilities of control are restricted to the devices for influencing thought, which are usually economic matters. Devices for control include prohibiting free exchange of ideas, or the mechanisms for censoring factual information and the expression of ideas. Hitler burned the books which seemed to him to interfere with the expansion of his power. In Russia there has been censorship of the Mendelian ideas of inherited traits. Unknown to most of the youth of Europe, due to censorship and neglect, are the concepts of a liberal society; these ideas are to them unknown rather than rejected, because one cannot reject an idea without knowing what it is. So it is only the range of choice that may be narrowed by the use of censorship.

"Freedom of the press" relates to the several means of transmitting ideas, which are mainly economic means. The issue of freedom of the press is fought over the right of a person to own and operate a newspaper, or to use newsprint, or in some other way to use economic goods and services in the transmitting of ideas to others.

"Freedom of speech" relates to the expressing of ideas to

others rather than the having of ideas. As a problem of liberty, it is closely akin to the right of assembly, where the censorship of speech takes the form of trying to break up assemblages of persons who would listen to a speaker. It is impossible to prevent these persons from thinking and believing what they will, but it is possible to control the use of places where the meetings might be held.

"Religious liberty" is ever secure. Since one's religious beliefs are a personal matter, the threat to liberty is restricted to the overt manifestations of religion — the church property where a meeting is to be held, the right to print and distribute literature, or the right to hire a specialist to teach matters of religious belief.

"Political liberty" is a problem only in connection with the expressing of political beliefs, rather than the having of these beliefs. It has to do with the usage of the political machine, and with the selection of those who will operate it. This political machine, however, operates mainly in matters of economics, and in that sense has to do with economic liberty rather than with liberty of beliefs. Votes buy things, and votes are bought.

Perhaps nowhere is the cause of liberty so much maligned as over these issues having to do with belief and ideas. One is prone to forget the personal nature of beliefs, with the result that other liberties are marauded in the futile effort to control something uncontrollable. We are prone to attack the professed beliefs of others with the weapon of power rather than reason. This complex problem of liberty as it relates to differences of opinion is, however, something aside from the main line of this discussion.

To whatever extent a person prevents the freedom of action of another, the liberty of that other person has suffered encroachment.

Two persons may desire to stand in the same place at the same time. This is a physical impossibility, and so long as both persist in their desires, the liberty of one or the other must suffer a loss. How can such problems be solved? Is there any way to preserve liberty in situations like that of two persons who may desire to stand in the same place at the same time, or who may bump into each other in other ways?

Physical relationships take many forms, among them being the outstandingly important one of "association." The hermit avoids the problem by associating with no one. But all except the hermit must face the problem of choice in association.

The only way to be totally "non-discriminating" in association with persons would be to share one's time and love equally among all persons on earth. As far as the time element of this plan is concerned, an average lifetime would allow a little less than one-half second of one's time for each other person.

Probably nobody wants to be a hermit. And total non-discrimination is a technical impossibility, even if one should desire to try it. So the problem of selection of associates is unavoidable; the question then becomes one of who shall have the rights of selection.

The selection of associates can be either by the person himself or for him by someone else. There is no other alternative.

Selection of associates by others can be illustrated by many commonplace events. A person in prison has his associates selected for him, for the duration of his stay. One who is forced to become a cog in a military machine, or who is assigned to civil tasks by a government that controls the labor force and employment, has lost his liberty in that realm of association. Parental or political selection of a spouse violates liberty in association, in a most important part of a person's life. Sometimes, for purposes of personal prestige or for other personal reasons, one may bring pressure to bear upon his spouse to join a club or a parent may make little Susie go to a party where the children in attendance are not to her liking. All these are instances of trespass on liberty in the matter of association.

Every voluntary association is a two-way deal, willingly accepted by both parties in the same manner as the free exchange of goods in the market place. The insistence of one person that another associate with him against the other's wishes is a violation of the other's liberty, in the same manner as forcing one to sell at a given price in the market place violates his liberty in that realm. In some of its more intimate forms, violating liberty of association is judged to be a criminal offense; but in other realms one is forced by law to violate his preferences as defined under liberty and freedom of choice — he is legally forced to "discriminate."

Under liberty, the right to select associates is sacred. One person may prefer to concentrate his association largely on one or a few other persons; another may prefer to scatter his association widely. There is no one "right" way to do it.

A person is not able to tell exactly why he selects certain persons as associates rather than others. If he cannot tell for himself, he is certainly unqualified to pass judgments for others. No person can have the insight into the preferences and wishes of another sufficient to justify his trying to manage these affairs for another. A parent probably knows his own child as well as one person can know another, yet attempts to judge the child's preferences in association usually end in utter failure.

Selection of associates is, to be sure, "discrimination." But if that right under liberty is to be judged improper or illegal, we shall have to make some drastic changes in our concepts about the propriety of monogamy, about the wisdom of several of the

Commandments, and about other important concepts of morals and justice in human society.

It is often falsely assumed that liberty in the choice of associates means irresponsibility in those relationships. But legal and non-legal contractual obligations, founded on free choice in the origin of the arrangement, can be made binding under liberty; forms with which we are familiar include marriage and employer-employee relationships. Contracts are not a violation of the tenets of liberty, but liberty requires that there be freedom of choice by the parties to the deal regarding the terms of the contract.

The only possible way to preserve liberty in physical relationships is to have acceptance of rules of the game such that situations of possible overlapping or conflicting desires are resolved in advance. What is needed is to have "rules for a ball game," such as those discussed in later sections, accepted by the players in advance. Acceptance of necessary and workable rules of the game prevents it from developing into mayhem. There is no other way by which the game of human relationships can be played without destroying the liberty of someone.

Surrender, forced upon one by the other, is not a solution consistent with liberty. It may serve as a truce during conflict, but that is all.

Forced arbitration, for the same reason, is not to be confused with a voluntary solution that is in harmony with liberty.

THE PROBLEM of economic liberty touches every exchange of goods and services, the ownership of property, and every contractual arrangement involving these "economic" affairs, because human relationships are involved in all of them.

Economic liberty is absent to whatever extent a person is prohibited from using his talents and his property to produce and sell (or exchange) anything he desires, at whatever price is agreeable to him and to the buyer. If he is prohibited from doing this, by another person or by any combination of persons who are not direct parties to the deal, his liberty is thereby transgressed. And further, it makes no difference, so far as liberty is concerned, under what name the act of prohibition is paraded; or whether it is by a corporation, a cooperative, a labor union, a trade union, the government, or what not.

Economic goods and services come into being as a result of the physical and mental acts of persons. Property and income have been called, quite appropriately, "the economic extensions of the person." What has been said about liberty in physical relationships, therefore, applies also to all economic affairs.

Economic affairs absorb a large part of all human thought and action, either directly or indirectly. If one considers carefully his every thought and action for a day, he will see that economics touches nearly every part. Although the most highly-prized things of life may be those beyond the economic pale — love, beauty, religious faith — the economic things of life tie in with most of these or are used in their behalf. Love may be expressed by gifts that are bought; intellectual enjoyment is aided by books; the trip to a religious meeting may be by auto or by train, to a meeting hall located on land owned by someone.

A high level of economic liberty is thus a requisite to all other liberties. Historical evidence shows that economic slaves enjoy none of these liberties, except as their masters may choose to allow a temporary slackening of their chains. The slave in old Rome, who is reported to have said to Caesar that he never really knew freedom until he became Caesar's slave, should have been the court jester; he exhibited a rare ability to compound foolishness!

A dictator who has full economic control over his subjects has in his hands the tools by which to deny them all other forms of alienable liberty, leaving them no recourse except rebellion.

The dictator can use economic means to deny any person a place to stand and speak his mind, and even a place to sit and think, merely by having control of all the land.

Thoreau, who attempted withdrawal from society in his pursuit of liberty, was caught and jailed for refusing to pay his taxes — a small handle with great powers over liberty.

Jan Masaryk, the Czechoslovakian patriot, was called a great defender of freedom. But he said: "... Czechoslovakia must work out the synthesis between Russian socialism and Western liberty ... I'll go all the way with Russia — all the way up to one point. Socialistic economics — okay. But if anyone tries to take away our freedom — freedom to think and say what you believe — the right to your own thoughts, your own soul. ..."

That was early in 1946. On March 10, 1948, after living for a time under the socialistic economics he had okayed, Masaryk plunged to his death from his office window in Prague. We may never know what induced him to suicide, but it may well have been that he came to realize the emptiness of his hope — the hope that persons can live in liberty after they have given up economic liberty.

It may be incorrect to say that economic liberty is the only form of liberty, but it seems correct to say that economic liberty pervades the entire problem of liberty and is an absolute requisite to liberty in general.

CHAPTER THREE

THE FOUNDATION
OF ECONOMIC LIBERTY

THE RIGHT OF A PERSON to the product of his own labor is the foundation of economic liberty. The requirements of liberty in the economic realm can be met in no other way.

The question at issue is how to distinguish between what is mine and what is thine. The hermit is not concerned about this matter, which becomes a problem only when two or more persons have relationships with one another.

There are three ways to handle this problem:

1. Each person may have whatever he can grab.

2. Some person other than the one who produces the goods and services may decide who shall have the right of possession or use.

3. Each person may be allowed to have whatever he produces.

These three methods cover all the possibilities; there are no others.

The first of these plans for distinguishing between mine and thine is the law of the jungle. It rests on the concept that might makes right; that the right of possession goes along with the strength and the power to take something from another. This method makes ownership hazardous and highly unstable. Under such a system, the one who produces anything faces the immediate danger that it will be taken from him against his will. It may then be stolen from the thief, and stolen again from the second thief — again and again until it has been consumed. An economy conducted in this manner will remain primitive, or will return to the primitive state, living largely on the "natural products" of the forests and the streams.

The law of the jungle discourages production and encourages consumption of even the little that is available; there is every urge to squander, and little or no incentive to thrift. He who would be enterprising, and who would create and use the tools of progress, is discouraged from doing so because of the likelihood that they will be taken from him by robbers. Wolves live in this manner; members of the pack subsist on what they can grab from the carcass of a sheep that has been pillaged from the farmer who reared it. An economy of this design will never build a Detroit, or a Radio City, or a great institution of research and learning. And it violates the tenets of liberty, for reasons which will be discussed later.

The second method of determining the rights of possession is the one on which every form of authoritarian society is founded, no matter what its name. According to this concept, someone other than the producer is empowered to decree who shall have whatever is produced. The means by which this person has gained this power, and the claims of "justice" which he attaches to his decrees, are not relevant at this point in the discussion. Sufficient for present purposes is the observation that he is empowered to confiscate that which others have produced, against the wishes of the producers, and to do with it as he chooses. It gives to the dictator, and to no one else, the right of spoliation; so it must be rejected as the design for a society wherein widespread liberty is to abound.

The only method consistent with liberty is the one that distinguishes between mine and thine according to the rule that the producer shall have the right to the product of his own labor. This foundation of economic liberty is important above all other considerations. By this concept, the right of ownership arises simultaneously with the production of anything; and ownership resides there until the producer-owner chooses to consume the product or to transfer its ownership to another person through exchange, gift or inheritance. The right to produce a thing thereby becomes the right to own it; and to deny one right is, in effect, to deny both. This concept specifies that no part of production shall properly belong to a thief, or to a slave master or to a ruler by whatever title.

Each of the first two concepts for distinguishing between mine and thine accepts the right of a non-producer to take from the producer the product of his labor; to that extent they are alike. The difference lies in whether the taking is to be a private matter or a "public" matter. Some claim that one is for selfish purposes and that the other is for unselfish purposes; that the thief takes things for his own consumption or use, whereas the dictator takes them in order to help his subjects. Capone is supposed to typify the first and Stalin the second. But all these distinctions are none too clear, and none too convincing as to any important difference. Robin Hood was supposed to have helped poor people with the fruits of his plunder; to which group should he belong? Some thieves are famed for their contributions to "worthy causes"; to which group should they belong? Many or most of the world's dictators and leading politicians have thickly feathered their own private nests with the proceeds of their public plunder; to which group should they belong? The one clear conclusion is that, from the viewpoint of the producer, his product has been taken from him against his wishes in both instances alike.

Those who are devoted to the second, or authoritarian, concept often confuse the first and third methods. They claim that both follow the law of the jungle. They fail to note the important distinction that the third method gives the person the right to the product of his own labor only, whereas the first gives him the right to grab that of his neighbor. In failing to note this most important distinction, and in rejecting both, these persons then advocate the only remaining alternative — the one which gives to a third party the right to take the product from both the producer and the robber. It is as though a widening of the range of take, so as to include the producer as well as the thief, somehow turns a vice into a virtue.

The method consistent with liberty, which gives a person the right to the product of his own labor — that and no more — gives everyone the same right so that no person is granted a license to trespass on the rights of others. It should be perfectly clear that if all persons are to have the right to the product of their own labor, they cannot in addition have claim to any of the product of another's labor; otherwise the rights of everyone will have been violated. There is no way to make the whole equal more than its parts. Geographic property rights, similarly, are destroyed whenever each person is allowed to move his legal boundary wherever he may choose.

The three concepts by which to distinguish between mine and thine have been defined in their pure forms, as they would operate wherever they are followed clearly, logically and without the confusion of dilution. Despite the current popularity of the "mixed economy" as a design for society, each person must accept as a principle of justice one or another of these three designs. In advocating and supporting another, either as part of a mixture or in pure form, he thereby surrenders his principle and engages in what his principles tell him will be economic self-destruction.

ANYTHING PRODUCED is property, and the question of the right to own property is automatically a part of the question of rights to whatever is produced.

The terms "immediate consumption" and "saving" are commonly used in contrast with one another. Their difference is one of time only, not of type. That which is kept a little longer than the other is said to have been "saved." The saving may be kept in kind, as wheat stored for winter; it may be sold, and the cash saved in a sock or in a bank or by putting it into some form of "investment" such as a farm or some other business.

The right of choice as to what is to be done with the product of one's labor is the whole purpose of having the right to it in the first place. If one should have the right to the product of his own labor — the foundation of economic liberty — it follows that he should have the right to do with it as he pleases; he may eat it now or later; he may keep it as an aid to further production; he may give it to others, to family, friends or organizations, now or later. To say that he shall be denied this full range of choice is to deny the essence of his basic right to the product of his own labor.

Permitting each person to take whatever he can grab is a complete denial of rights to private property. What the robber is thereby entitled to possess is the property of the one robbed.

The authoritarian concept likewise denies the right to private property. Its violation of liberty is commonly camouflaged by enticing labels. It is claimed under this plan that "everything shall be owned by everyone," with "ownership in common." In reality, the dictator alone holds the right of ownership, because he alone can do with it as he wishes. The corollary of the right of ownership is the right of disownership. If a private citizen is prohibited from selling or consuming his share of what is "owned in common," it is proof of the fact that he did not really have the rights of ownership in the first place.

Little progress could ever have occurred anywhere in the world without the right of a person to own private property. And continued progress requires full protection of this right.

Apparently nine-tenths or more of the economic welfare in the more prosperous nations of the world results from the use of the accumulated tools of production rather than from human effort unaided by these tools. The arts and other non-economic forms of progress, in turn, depend on a degree of economic welfare that will allow these products of leisure to be developed without imposing starvation on one's self and his family.

The tools that are necessary for economic prosperity and for "cultural progress" will not be accumulated except as the person who saves them is assured of continuing rights to their possession, as a storehouse for his savings. Attempts of the past to "force" persons to save under some plan by which rights of ownership belong solely to the master or to the one that governs the people have met an early failure. Saving ends, and past savings are consumed in an attempt to prevent a decline in the level of living.

Persons save for themselves and for those they love and respect, not for others neither known nor respected as worthy. They do not save for others unknown and for uses unknown, beyond their control. When private property is in constant danger of being taken from the one who has saved it, he will "eat today's production today" rather than save. If the marauding is prevalent enough, he will not even find it feasible to save the seed for next year's planting of food crops; and once the incentive to save is that far gone, civilization will have reverted back to the hunter society of primitive man.

It would seem, then, that the claim of one renowned person who said: "Only well-fed people can be free," could more accurately be stated in reverse: "Only free people can be well-fed."

Economic liberty prevails only if the individual person is

permitted to save in the form of private property, and to use it as he sees fit. The famous philosopher Hume believed the right of private ownership of property to be the basis of the modern concept of justice in morals.[1] His belief deserves careful consideration.

Satisfying one's wants with the least possible effort is the basic economic urge; it is the economic equivalent of the geometric concept that a straight line is the shortest distance between two points.

If this basic urge is unrestrained by morals, and by the foresight of consequences flowing from various methods of satisfying one's immediate wants, the course of least effort is likely to seem to be that of stealing the food and things from one's neighbor. Animals, lacking these moral and intellectual restraints, act in that manner and live by marauding. Man's higher order of intelligence and foresight has codified into written and unwritten law a restraint from short-sighted fulfillment of his wants by marauding. He has established privateness of property, and stabilization of the rights of its possession. Under the intellectual and moral code of advanced forms of human society, man acts differently from these "lower animals"; and he can continue to live in an advancing society only so long as that code of conduct is not undermined and allowed to fall.

Of all the essentials for the establishment of an advancing human society, the right to private property, as a moral concept, seems fundamental. Socialism means: "A state or a system in which there is no private property." Yet advocates of socialism claim for it the virtue of its being a system of society advanced beyond that of liberalism and rights to private property. How could socialism be an advanced form, when it embraces a concept that would have precluded the advancement of civilization?

[1] Henry D. Aiken, *Hume's Moral and Political Philosophy* (New York: Hafner Publishing Company, 1948), Book III.

The only advancement to be claimed for socialism is its advancement in the sense of time because, due to its inability to generate any accumulation of the tools required for an advanced society, it must subsist on the confiscation of what has already been produced under some other plan; it has to parasitize something. The confiscation of private property is civilization in retreat.

Is there any aspect of what may properly be called human justice that does not rest in one way or another, as Hume said, on the concept of rights to private property? Rights to private property are human rights; it is not a question of "human rights or property rights" as is frequently asserted.

In the analysis thus far it has been concluded:

1. That liberty is a human right, unlimited except as it is necessary to restrain one person from trespassing on the liberty of another (as will be discussed in later chapters).

2. That economic liberty is the safeguard of other forms of liberty, and apparently essential to their preservation.

3. That the right to the product of one's labor is the foundation of economic liberty.

4. That the right to private ownership of property follows from the right to the product of one's labor, because it is the inseparable "time aspect" of that right.

Thus, by successive steps, there is established a direct connection between property rights and human rights. The connection is one of harmony rather than of conflict. And one who would assert them to be in opposition to one another, and who speaks of "human rights or property rights," must identify the point in this series of deductions where he would disagree.

Does he believe that liberty is inhuman rather than human, as a matter of rights; that a demonstration of "human rights" is to be found in the slave auctions of early days, or in the slave camps of modern Russia?

If not, does he believe that an economic slave is likely to be allowed to enjoy the other forms of liberty, and that it is those other forms that comprise the "human rights"?

If not, does he believe that economic liberty means prohibiting a person from having the product of his own labor?

If not, does he believe that a person can have the right to the product of his labor while being denied the right to keep any of it even for an instant?

If he believes none of these, he must believe that rights to private property are inseparably entwined with human rights.

Dwight D. Eisenhower, on the occasion of his induction as President of Columbia University, listed the private ownership of property as one of four "cherished rights" of persons. He said further that these rights are mutually dependent for their existence, without which human rights would soon disappear.

Any Bill of Human Rights that excludes the right to private property is doomed to futility and failure.

CHAPTER FOUR

LIBERTY AND CHARITY

IT IS NEITHER POSSIBLE nor feasible to discuss here all the many accusations that may be directed at the author's definition of liberty, and at the foundation of economic liberty as it has been identified. But one accusation above all others seems to have wide appeal, and deserves some attention in even this brief treatment of the subject of liberty; it is the charge that liberty means selfishness and a lack of the spirit of charity.

Is liberty, as defined, in conflict with charity? Is it proper to accuse one who asserts his right to the product of his own labor, together with rights to private property, of being uncharitable and totally self-seeking? Those who hold the affirmative view, in answer to these questions, argue that "liberty" should include the right of one person to take from another the product of his labor for purposes of "charity."

The right to the product of one's own labor, and the associated right to keep it and to do with is as one may choose, is not in conflict with compassion and charity. Leaving these matters to voluntary action, rather than to apply compulsion, is in harmony rather than in conflict with Christian ethics. The distinction between the two ideas is this: assistance given voluntarily and anonymously from the product of one's own labor, or from his property that has been saved, is truly charity; that taken from another by force, on the other hand, is not charity at all, in spite of its use for avowed "charitable purposes." The virtue of compassion and charity cannot be sired by the vice of thievery.

"Political charity" violates the essentials of charity in more ways than one. It is not anonymous; on the contrary, there is boasting about the process by the politician both in the form of campaign promises yet unfilled as well as by reminders during the term of office; this is intended to insure that the receiver of these fruits of "charity" is kept mindful of an enduring obligation to the political agent. And the source of the giving is not from the pocket of the political giver himself, who has already violated the requirement of anonymity for purposes of personal gain; the wherewithal is taken by force from the pockets of others. And some of the amount collected is deducted for "costs of administering" by the one who claims personal virtue in the process. All told, the process of "political charity" is about as complete a violation of the requisites of charity as can be conceived.

Those who contend that the rights of liberty are in conflict with charity falsely assume that persons generally have a total disregard for the welfare of others, and that widespread starvation would result from liberty as thus defined. Evidence to the contrary is that the infant and the helpless members of the family, and other needy persons, do not ordinarily starve in a society where these rights prevail. The right to have income and private property means the right to control its disposition and use; it does not mean that the person himself must consume it all himself.

A matter deserving of thought, but which will be little more than posed as a question in this discussion, is that of the effect on compassion when welfare by force is attempted as a substitute for charity; when aid is no longer that of voluntary and anonymous donations from the product of one's labor, for specific and known purposes.

Compassion is a purely personal thing. The body politic cannot have compassion. One cannot delegate compassion to a hired agent. Nor is compassion so cheap a virtue as to be practiced by the mere distributing of grants of aid taken from the pockets of others, rather than from one's own pocket or from his own effort in production. A charity worker may be a kindly and lovable soul, but as far as compassion is concerned, he is only an employed person buying groceries and things for certain persons by using other people's money, in a manner like that of the housemaid who goes shopping for her employer.

Under a scheme of affairs where a political body takes full responsibility in the caring for the victims of disaster, it is doubtful if compassion can long endure. When a taxpayer is forced to contribute to "charity" in spite of his judgment of need, he will increasingly shun the sense of responsibility which is requisite to a spirit of compassion; he will lose compassion as he more and more accepts the viewpoint: "That is the government's business!"

Once compassion is lost on a wholesale basis in a nation, how is it ever to be regained? And once it is gone, what will then happen to the attitude of responsibility for supporting the churches and all other similar agencies which depend on voluntary support?

Advocacy of these rights of liberty is sometimes called "selfishness." "Self," if used in this sense, means the entire circle of the person's family, friends, relatives, organizations — anything which this person considers worthy of help from his income or savings.

If "selfishness" is to be charged against the one who demands the right to that which he has produced, selfishness of a far less virtuous order should also be charged against any non-producer who takes the income and wealth from another against his will.

If control of the disposition and use of income and wealth is to be called "selfishness," then it is unavoidable that someone act selfishly in the handling of everything produced. The question then becomes: Who should have the right to be selfish, the one who produced it or some other person? Is it selfishness to control the disposition of that which you have produced, but unselfish to control the disposition of that which you have taken from those who produced it?

For this argument to be accepted, one would have to hold that non-producers are better qualified than producers to judge the wise use of what is produced. He would have to hold that non-producers are somehow more virtuous than producers; that they have superior wisdom and conscience. He would have to hold that the taking away from the producer by force will not discourage him from production, since it is not possible to be charitable with something not produced.

The late Justice Oliver Wendell Holmes once said that someone must exercise command of the disposition of goods and services that have been produced, and that he knew of no way of finding the fit man so good as the fact of winning it in the competition of the market.

If the members of the human race be so self-centered that they are judged to be unqualified to handle the use of what they have labored to produce, the advocates of "charity" by force — whether operated by a thief or by a dictator — must face an interesting question. How will it be possible to administer the program? Who can be found to operate a program of "wise charity," if that be true? If one could be found, by what respectable means could he be expected to gain his throne of power over all those supposedly self-centered dregs of humanity? Anyone who would pursue this evasive hope should read Professor F. A. Hayek's brilliant chapter, "Why the Worst Get on Top," in his book The Road to Serfdom.

They should also review Lord Acton's famous dictum about the corrupting influence of power. And finally, they should review carefully their starting assumption that justice and charity and selflessness can best be attained through giving legal or moral sanction to the taking by one person of the product of another's labor by force. Whence comes the alleged superiority in the morals and wisdom of the taker — is it the result of his having engaged in the taking, or in gaining power over others, or from where? More reasonable is the assumption that proficiency in these respects is found in a person lacking in morals and wisdom.

Liberty is not in conflict with charity. More accurately, charity is possible and can reach large proportions only under liberty; and under liberty, "need" for it would probably be greatly reduced.

CHAPTER FIVE

RULES OF CONDUCT IN A LIBERAL SOCIETY

LIBERTY HAS BEEN DEFINED in this discussion as a strictly individual matter. Further, as a problem of our concern, it has been limited to the area where relationships exist between persons, "society."

All who favor liberty, therefore, must favor the liberal society. They must favor "liberalism" (liber = free; al = pertaining to; ism = a doctrine or practice).

The structure of a liberal society is that which promises to preserve the greatest possible degree of liberty among those living in that society. The design of a liberal society requires the formulation of rules, acceptable to the participants, that will accomplish this purpose. The rules must apply to all situations where overlapping desires might otherwise arise to destroy liberty, such as when two persons desire to stand in the same place at the same time. Under adequate rules accepted by the participants, each will refrain from trespassing on the rights of others. The rules for conduct in society are accepted in the same spirit and with the same respect as a person accepts the dictates of physical law where the connection between cause and effect, between the breaking of the law and its consequences, is fairly conspicuous.

If the rules of the game are to be acceptable to the participant, they must be in accord with his sense of justice. But this sense of justice must, in turn, be in harmony with sound principles. "Just any old rules" will not suffice, because if in their operation they fail to perform their purpose in coping with the problems that continuously arise, respect for them will end and they will be rejected by the participant.

Under liberty, one person has no inherent right to control another. One person may influence another by appeal to his wisdom and conscience without violating liberty, because self-control and self-restraint are respected guides to action under liberty. Everyone is, in effect, a sworn-in policeman over his own acts; conscience allows neither evasion nor escape from self-responsibility.

This concept of liberty rests on the supreme dignity of the individual. Shunning responsibility for one's own acts is impossible because no one else has control over him with responsibility for his acts. Rights under liberty have their counterpart in duties under liberty.

Liberty (freedom to do whatever one desires according to his wisdom and conscience) in no sense means that one must ignore all the experience of the ages and wisdom of the sages. Evidence and guidance which one person chooses to accept from another, or from recorded history, is no violation of liberty. Liberty does not preclude learning from others. On the contrary, the absence of liberty prevents the process of free access to others and the free exchange of ideas.

One who chooses to accept all the accumulated knowledge of the ages as interpreted by his physician is free, under liberty, to accept his physician's advice and buy his pills. But liberty also allows him to patronize either of the two physicians who differ as to the possible cure; or it allows him to patronize neither and to be his own doctor.

The same reasoning applies to all other human relationships, and to the designing of rules of conduct in a liberal society. Intellectual and moral guidance, voluntarily accepted by the follower, is no violation of liberty; it is, in fact, a main purpose of liberty so that the blind are free to follow those who can see. The danger is that in the absence of liberty the blind may become authorized to lead those who can see — by a chain around their necks!

The terrific urge to prevent another person from making a "mistake" must be resisted if liberty is to be preserved. The "protective spirit" that leads a fond parent to prohibit his child from acquiring mature judgments, as he substitutes his own opinions for those of the child, leads the dictator to act as he does in "protecting" his political children. There is no possible way to allow a person to be right without also allowing him to be wrong. The only way to avoid responsibility for another's mistakes is to allow him the full glory and reward of being right, as well as the full dishonor and penalty of being wrong. Only in this way can one person isolate himself from the mistakes of another, whether it be a Stalin or a neighbor.

The rules of a liberal society must be in harmony with those forces beyond the power of man to alter, where any violation brings certain penalty. Similar forces prevent the mathematician from having the license to decree that two plus two is five or three; in observing these superior forces of truth, he is thus protected from a whole series of impossible mathematical situations. And similarly, the engineer and the physicist, if they are to avoid disaster in their projects, must work in harmony with the law of gravity rather than in defiance of it. The mathematician, physicist and engineer all know that they are not God with an unlimited control over matter and over "truth."

There are forces of a similar nature that cannot be defied in the conduct of a liberal society, if disastrous results are to be avoided. It is impossible, for instance, to grant to everyone a valid right to use whatever land he desires, at any time; it is inadvisable to permit plunder and pillage. Any such attempts to flout natural and moral law will bring disaster to liberty and to the society that practices it. It is not intended to propose here a complete listing of the "natural moral laws" requisite to liberalism. But it is at least important to note their existence and to suggest their nature.

The Golden Rule — the rule of doing unto others what one would have them do unto him — would seem to be one requisite of the code of liberalism. This is because, in the moral realm, the Golden Rule serves the necessary function of impartiality; it is no respecter of privileged persons, not even one's esteemed self. It is the equivalent of the impartiality of rule by law instead of rule according to the whims of the administrators.

But the Golden Rule alone is not sufficient. Lacking any other moral guides, the Golden Rule may even be used to rationalize thievery; the thief may claim in self-defense: "If I were in the victim's place, having two cars, I would be willing to have someone without a car take one of mine." Additional guides such as the Ten Commandments, or perhaps the Cardinal Sins, are necessary.

A set of rules, thus properly designed and accepted, is the requisite of a liberal society. When this objective is attained, liberty will be complete and undefiled in a society where persons are constantly engaged in all sorts of economic and other relationships with one another.

Such a set of rules prescribes the range of a person's actions in his relationships with others which, if observed by him and by others alike, allows full liberty to be enjoyed by all. Each knows that he is free to operate over a certain range and no more; if he is not free to operate over this range, he can be assured that others are imposing on his liberty; if he exceeds this range, he will know that he is infringing on the liberty of others. Such is the nature of liberal justice, without which liberty cannot be preserved.

Liberty, or the right to act as one wills according to his wisdom and conscience, is sometimes charged with being "license" and totally irresponsible conduct. But, on the contrary, responsibility of the highest order is required in a liberal society. What social design could be more challenging, in terms of responsibility, self-discipline and self-control, than that of liberalism in its requirements of self-restraint; in avoiding trespass on the rights and the property of others; in its respect for the rights of others to disagree without precipitating conflict? Liberty requires the highest order of conduct in its practice.

The disciplines of liberty, however, have their rewards. "Every man a king" has had great appeal as a political slogan. The nearest possible approach to it is to be found in a liberal society, in which everyone is king over his own affairs to the greatest possible extent. At the other extreme, one man is king over all men instead of every man being king to a degree.

RULES OF SOCIETY come into existence in different ways. Whereas this study deals primarily with government in its relation to liberty, it may be helpful to note briefly the other devices for developing the rules of society. Their record in attaining the ideal of liberalism varies throughout history, and the record of no one of them seems to offer a panacea.

Presumably the earliest rules for social conduct were those developed in the family, as an early social unit. They differed from family to family, but in all instances they were informal and easily changed.

Perhaps next in time of origin was "custom." Custom operated to develop rules of society in the same manner as Topsy developed

— they "just grew up." Custom is an unwritten code of conduct, voluntarily accepted and enforced by self-discipline, assisted by the frowns and the approving smiles of friends and neighbors. The force of custom has been terrific at different times and places. But it is not a certain route to liberty, in any sense, though there is an important virtue to be found in its voluntary nature.

Both religious belief and the operations of the organized religious bodies have played an important role in designing rules of social conduct. They have varied; some have been formal and others informal; some voluntary and others users of force; some with rewards and penalties imposed here and others merely promised for the hereafter; some independent of government and others in collusion with government.

Many forms of social and fraternal organizations, operating as cells within society, have also established rules of conduct for their members.

In earlier days, the tribe was important in formulating rules for social conduct. In modern times, "government" has to a large extent replaced the functions of the tribal organization, and has become a major factor in the development and enforcement of rules for social conduct. Because of its growing importance and its threat to liberty, government is given special attention in this study.

CHAPTER SIX

GOVERNMENT IN A LIBERAL SOCIETY

ONE OF THE MOST perplexing problems of the ages seems to have been that of finding the proper place of government in society.

Like any of the powers in the physical world, government is at once a power for good and a power for evil. Considerable success has attended man's efforts to use wisely the power contained in coal, oil, and the waterfalls. But the power of government in social affairs, like the newly developed atomic power in the physical world, still is an untamed and unharnessed force of great danger; and the supreme danger of our time is that these two forces may be combined somewhere in the world — even in our own country — as a force for evil.

The place of government as an agency empowered to intercede in the affairs of individuals may be thought of in the same way as the right of a person to own private property. In both instances there are limits to the scope of rights. A person's rights to private property are specific, clearly identified and limited — which is precisely the reason for the establishing of rights to private property. Similarly with government; to concede that there is a purpose in having a government with certain powers is not to concede that

THE NATURE OF GOVERNMENT [49]

the scope of governmental power over the affairs of individuals should be all-inclusive, or that one power justifies another.

Government is a legalized entity. To view government aside from the persons who comprise it and aside from the personal powers they hold is to view an empty shell — or perhaps more accurately, it is to view "nothing wrapped in nothingness." Thus it follows without exception that any power of government means, in reality, that certain persons are empowered to do something to certain other persons. It cannot be otherwise. In judging the propriety of any specific issue of governmental power, an aid in answering it might be to reformulate the question as follows: Is it proper for this person (or persons) to do this thing to this other person (or persons)?

Government is, by definition, design and intent, an agency engaged in force. It is not necessary, for instance, to empower government to decree that the citizens shall eat when they are hungry, or sing and be thankful when they are happy, or to do any of the innumerable other things that free individuals do voluntarily. Government is engaged in issuing laws and decrees, and in their enforcement. Government conducts "war" on outsiders and "law enforcement" on insiders. Its purpose and operation is well characterized by the statement: "There ought to be a law. . . ." Its operations involve force or the threat of force against certain persons, thus violating the liberty of those persons.

As is well known in our time, a government may be totally tyrannical. An all-powerful government, wherein all the citizens are under the heel of a dictator, allows no liberty to anyone except the dictator himself. It has been said that the authoritarian society is one wherein everything not prohibited is compulsory. The dictator may, of course, grant temporary privileges to some in the same manner as a prison warden grants privileges to a "trusty."

Based on all that has been said, one might easily conclude

that government is an entirely negative force so far as liberty is concerned. He might conclude that anarchy — the complete absence of government — would be the ideal society, and that liberty would be complete under anarchy. That would be true if all persons were perfect. But they are not. With human frailties as they are, anarchy affords an opportunity for certain powerful and tyrannical individuals to enslave their fellow men, to the extent of their power to gain and keep control over others. So some degree of governmental function — or its equivalent performed in some other way — is necessary if liberty is to be at a maximum; violators of liberty must be restrained so that the rights of liberty will be protected for those who respect them and play the game of society according to the rules of liberalism.

Thus at one extreme the absence of government allows anarchy to rob the people of their liberty, whereas at the other extreme the government itself becomes the robber of liberty. The task in a liberal society, therefore, is to find that point where all the people will enjoy the greatest possible degree of liberty. It will allow full enjoyment of liberty by all who refrain from going beyond their rights and imposing on the liberty of others. Those who violate this trust of rights under liberty, and who destroy the liberty of others in addition, shall be forced as a penalty for their avarice to give up their own liberty, in whole or in part, depending on their crime against liberty.

In the liberal society, any coercive power is viewed with suspicion, whether its growth has been attained in the form of business monopolies, labor monopolies or government — which by its very nature is coercive and monopolistic. To government should be delegated, of course, the powers necessary to preserve a maximum of liberty under limited, precise law. Up to that point, government is an instrument that increases liberty throughout society; beyond that point, government reduces the liberty of the people.

A simple case may serve to illustrate the possible effects of government on liberty. Assume a society of two persons. One has enslaved the other, so that there is an average of 50 per cent slavery and 50 per cent liberty in that society $\left(\frac{100 + 0}{2}\right)$.[1] Now assume that the slaveholder somehow becomes convinced that the slave should be freed, and voluntarily frees him, thus allowing the society to operate so that the liberty of neither of the persons is curbed in any degree; the level of liberty would then rise to 100 per cent $\left(\frac{100 + 100}{2}\right)$. If, however, it should be necessary by force of government to restrict the liberty of the former slaveholder by 10 per cent in order to restrain him from imposing on his fellow countryman, the average level of liberty would be 95 per cent $\left(\frac{90 + 100}{2}\right)$ — and under that assumption a 95 per cent liberty would be the maximum attainable in that society. The government, if it should exceed its proper scope and functions, might further reduce the average level of liberty unnecessarily to 90 per cent, 80 per cent, . . . , 0 per cent.

Government may then serve as an agency to maintain liberty at the highest point possible, or it may restrict liberty even to the point of its near-complete destruction.

The definition of liberty as it applies to a society of persons might be restated as follows: A liberal society is one in which,

[1] The term slavery will be used in the ensuing sections as the antonym for liberty. It is a shocking word to most of us, but it must be admitted that the opposite of liberty is a shocking condition.

In visualizing slavery in terms of a perspiring slave, toiling in chains under the lash of a master's whip while bloodhounds in the background guard against his escape, it should be noted that the form of slavery of which this discussion will speak as the problem of our day is slavery even in the absence of the whip and the bloodhounds. It is more subtle and inconspicuous than the older form. This newer form of slavery may be present or absent in varying degrees, but it is still slavery in the essential meaning of that word — the opposite of liberty and freedom.

So the word slavery, with all its frightening qualities, seems best to fit the condition being discussed.

with equality under law for all persons, each person can do most nearly that which is his wish according to his wisdom and conscience.

Under a government consistent with liberalism, the maximum of personal liberty that is attainable depends on the degree of human frailties; the persons who commit the crimes against liberty are the ones compelled to pay the penalty, as with all justice. A government of liberalism, be it noted with emphasis, is not one whose officials and employees are dined, wined and eulogized for "statesmanship" as a reward for having contributed to the destruction of liberty!

CHAPTER SEVEN

DEMOCRACY AND LIBERTY

IT IS GENERALLY ACCEPTED that a government can enslave the citizens. Enough Kings and Emperors and Generalissimos and Führers have done so to establish that fact quite conclusively.

But the belief prevails that: "It is impossible for liberty to be lost under a democratic form of government. Democracy assures that the will of the people shall prevail, and that is liberty. So long as democracy is preserved we can rest assured that liberty will be continued to the full."

The more a person leans on an unsure support the more certain he is to fall. Edmund Burke observed that people never give up their liberties except under some delusion. Probably no other belief is now so much a threat to liberty in the United States and in much of the rest of the world as the one that democracy, by itself alone, guarantees liberty.

Willis Ballinger's study of eight great democracies of the past — ancient Athens, Rome, Venice, Florence, the First and Third Republics of France, Weimar Germany and Italy — reveals how unreliable is this hope.[1] He reports that liberty perished peacefully

[1] Willis J. Ballinger, *By Vote of the People* (New York: Charles Scribner's Sons, 1946).

by vote of the people in five of the eight countries; that in two of them it was lost by violence; that in one of them a dictatorship was established through the buying of the legislature by a fraudulent clique. One who would understand the problem of liberty must understand why it is possible for liberty to be lost even in a democracy, and how to guard against it.

The "democratic" form of government refers to one of the mechanisms by which the scope of government — the things to be done by government — is to be determined and how its management is to be selected. This may be done directly by decisions of the people themselves (in a "direct" or "absolute" democracy), as when a direct vote is taken on an amendment; or it may be done by delegating the power of decision in these matters to certain "elected" representatives (in a "representative" democracy or "republic"). There is an important difference between these two types of democracy but that distinction is not the object of our present concern.

In both instances, the plan rests on widespread sovereignty at its base. Decisions as to either the issues or the delegations of power are rendered according to the majority — or some other predominant proportion — of the opinions expressed.

The features that distinguish a democracy from any other form of government have to do with the mechanical design of the government, as distinguished from the composition of the load of authority which it carries. This is the same sort of difference as that of the design of a truck as distinguished from its load, or the shape of a cup as distinguished from its contents. In speaking of liberty, what we are really concerned about is what government does — the nature of the load — rather than the style of wheels on which it rides, or some other feature in the design of the vehicle; we are concerned, for instance, with whether or not the government should control prices rather than the department which shall do the job or the name of the person who is to head the department.

If an act of government in any country violates the liberty of the people, it is of little importance who did it or how he came to have the power to do it; it is of little importance whether a dictator gained his power by accident of birth, by force, or by the vote of the people.

Liberty has been defined as the right of a person to do whatever he desires, according to his wisdom and conscience. It specifies the right to do what he desires, rather than the obligation to bow to the force of others in doing what they desire him to do; otherwise slavery becomes "liberty," and true liberty is lost. It makes no difference whether the transgressor of liberty carries the title of slave master, or King, or Führer, or President, or Chairman of the County Committee, or what not.

Historical enterprises which violate liberty are not restricted to instances of complete dictatorship, nor are they all political. The only difference between the aggressive bully under anarchy and the similar acts of the dictator is its formalization into governmental authority. That may make the acts of the dictator legal, in a technical sense, but it does not make them proper or wise in any other sense.

Small dictatorships precede large ones, and destroy liberty to whatever extent they exist. "Power," which replaces liberty, is the irrevocable authority over others. One person's opinions, decisions or actions become substituted for those of another, for a long or short time, for a wide or narrow scope. This is the material of which dictatorships, either large or small, are made. The means by which power is acquired, whether by the "democratic" process or by conquest, does not change its status as power. It is true that under persuasion or demonstration, one person may influence the ideas or actions of another; but, as mentioned before, if there is no irrevocable grant of authority — even temporarily or for one single instance — it is not power.

Suppose, as illustration of encroachment on liberty, that I desire to produce some wheat on my land, with which to feed my family. I shall have lost my liberty in that connection whenever I am prohibited from doing so. The loss of liberty would be the same whether the prohibition was by taking my land, or by prohibiting me from growing wheat on it, or by taking the wheat away from me after it was grown. Nor would it make any difference what official title happened to be attached to the person who enforced the edict, nor how he gained his throne of authority. Further, and most important to the subject now under discussion, it makes no difference whether or not some of my neighbors approved of that act, or how many of them approved of it. It makes no difference because, in any event, my liberty in this respect would be gone.

It should be clear from what has been said that the citizens of a democracy have in their hands the tools by which to enslave themselves.

This is a far cry from the common belief that democracy offers any definite and automatic protection of liberty. This illusion, that the democratic process is the same as liberty, is an ideal weapon for those few who may desire to destroy liberty and to replace it with some form of authoritarian society; innocent but ignorant persons are thereby made their dupes. Under the spell of this illusion, liberty is most likely to be lost and its loss not discovered until too late. Liberty can easily be taken from the individual citizen, piece by piece and always more and more, as more and more persons under the spell of the same illusion join in the Pied Piper proceedings. Finally, all liberty is gone and can be recovered only by a bloody revolution.

LIBERTY DOES NOT MEAN the right to do anything that is the product of a democratic form of government. The right to vote, which is the sovereignty feature of democracy, assures only the liberty to participate in that process. It does not assure that everything done by that process shall automatically be in the interests of liberty. A populace may commit both political and economic suicide under a democracy.

Anyone who will defend his liberty must guard against the argument that access to the ballot, "by which people get whatever they want," is liberty. It would be as logical to assert that liberty in the choice of a wife is assured to a person if he will put it to the vote of the community and accept their plurality decision, or that liberty in religion is assured if the state enforces participation in the one religion that receives the most votes in the nation.

There is no certainty whatever that liberty in a country with the democratic form of government is at a level higher than in a country having some other mechanism of government. There is no certainty that liberty will be maintained where the founders of a democracy may have hoped that it would be preserved.

The illusion that liberty is assured so long as a democratic government is preserved is well illustrated by an event reported in the newspaper. Items to illustrate the same point can be found in the newspapers daily. A news dispatch reports that an increase in rent ceilings has been "turned down" by "top administration officials." The mere fact that some officials have acquired the power to deny this liberty to those who own this particular form of property is evidence of the fact that liberty in this respect is already gone; no process of selecting the officials who made the decision can make it not gone.

But let us pursue the matter further. It is argued that, since this act occurred in a "democracy," the "will of the people" has prevailed and liberty has thereby been assured. Did you participate in this decision of "top officials"? Did anyone ever ask your opinion about whether this increase should be granted? Was the person who made the decision elected by the voters, or appointed by someone — perhaps by someone who was himself appointed by someone? And finally, coming to the elected official, did you vote for him or for the other fellow? Did you approve of his advisers, or were they perhaps defeated candidates-for-office of former years? Actually all these considerations are beside the point anyhow, so far as liberty is concerned. Even if there had been approval all along the line, it is a violation of economic liberty and of liberty in general for me, a non-owner, to be able to control the rent charged by a neighbor to a third party.

Being able to review a decision or to request its review, under the democratic design of government, does not assure that liberty will be protected. Reinstatement of lost liberty can be requested and refused time and time again, without end. A slave, similarly, might ask his master for his freedom time and time again; he is not considered to be free by reason of the fact that he is allowed to ask for liberty.

Consider in detail all the acts of all the units of government for one day. How many among them were the proper functions of a liberal government as you would judge it; of those that were, in how many instances did you have any opportunity or right to participate in the decision; if you disagreed with the decision, in how many instances was there anything that you could do about it?

Strange indeed is this concept of "democratic liberty" which has gained such widespread approval! Strange is a concept of "liberty" which allows you to be forced to pay the costs of promoting acts of which you disapprove or ideas with which you disagree, or which forces you to subsidize that which you consider to be slothfulness and negligence. Your "liberty" in the process is that you enjoy the right to be forced to bow to the dictates of others, against your wisdom and conscience! Being forced to support things directly in conflict with one's wisdom and conscience is the direct opposite of liberty, and should under no circumstances be allowed to parade under the esteemed banner of liberty. It should be labelled for what it is.

The people of the United States now live under a President who was elected to that office by the expressed preference of only one person out of six in the land; by only one person out of four who were eligible to vote; by less than half of those who voted. And many of those who voted for this candidate will certainly disapprove of many of his official acts. This illustrates how the democratic process is a far cry from guaranteeing the liberty of the people.

It was said that Hitler was elected to power by a minor expression of preference of the German people in a free election — which certainly did not assure liberty to the German people! Even though the vote in a free election had been unanimous for Hitler, the destruction of liberty might have been even more rapid.

It will be argued that some government is necessary to prevent the loss of liberty through anarchy; that the liberty of certain individuals should be curbed in the interests of liberty for all; that the scope of government must somehow be decided, and that the officials must somehow be selected; that no better means is available than that of widespread franchise. I agree. For those matters that are the functions of government in a liberal society, and in the selection of the persons to operate it, the test of dominant preference is probably the safest. But it is not a cure-all for the troubles of society because it does not compensate for those human frailties which are the sole source of any need for government in the first place.

Government of even the best design should be used only where, in the interests of liberty, it becomes necessary to arrive at a singleness in pattern of conduct. This problem of variation in relation to progress will be discussed in the following section.

The maximum of liberty is the maximum of democracy, if by democracy is meant the right of a person to have control over his own affairs. To whatever extent one person gains control over the affairs of another, that other person thereby loses his democratic rights in this sense. This is why the expansion of governmental activities beyond those in harmony with liberalism destroys these democratic rights, even though in a "democracy" there has been granted the widespread right to vote. All minorities are thereby disfranchised from their democratic rights in this sense, because their wishes become overruled in the process. Minorities become the slaves of the others, just as the inmates of Hitler's Germany became his slaves. Participation in these steps that make it possible for someone to rule others does not ensure liberty.

It is fantastic nonsense to assert that the democratic process will assure liberty to the individuals of any nation, whatever the other arguments in its favor. So long as this illusion prevails, it would be more accurate to say that it is a most certain path to slavery.

Decision by the test of dominant preference (majority vote, etc.) is the same operating principle as the one that might makes right. If might makes right, one must conclude that liberty is all wrong.

The test of whether or not a government is defending liberty is to be found in what it does, never in the mechanics of its operation. The test is whether or not the officials in any government, as well as the content of the laws and regulations, are in harmony or in conflict with the requirements of liberty as previously defined.

CHAPTER EIGHT

VARIATION AND PROGRESS

LIBERTY GIVES a unique form of satisfaction for which there is no substitute. And furthermore, liberty is the environment wherein the seeds of progress can sprout and bear fruit, for all to share who will.

What are the seeds of progress, and why does liberty offer the environment for their development? The contrast between humans and other forms of life may offer a clue to the answer.[1]

The Maker, we may assume, has a purpose in such differences that exist between various forms of life. This is evidenced by the fact that these differences exist. What is the special destiny, or purpose, of the human form of life?

The purpose is not clearly a matter of survival. Humans have no special claim to that blessing. Other forms of life have continued to survive, and presumably most of them will continue to do so.

The contrast between humans and other forms of life, suggesting the features with which humans have been especially

[1] For a more technical discussion of this contrast, see: Ernest N. Cory, "Totalitarian Insects," address of the President, American Association of Economic Entomologists, Journal of Economic Entomology, Feb., 1948.

endowed, might be found by contrasting them with trees or some other form of plant life. But it seems best to contrast some form of mobile life that operates in a manner more closely related to the problem under discussion — liberty. The social insects seem to serve that purpose well.

Much of the following discussion is, of necessity, a matter of speculation based on what seems to be known about these insects and about humans, and about the various biological processes such as "natural selection." One's certainty in speculating on these matters is limited by never having been a bee, and by not having been a bee among the bees of a few million years ago.

AN ANCIENT Russian myth asserts that ants were once men — the first experimental design of men. They developed as systems, not as individuals. In the development of this "perfectly planned society," every minute detail was plotted. In this classless society, each ant-man had at birth an appointed place. He was not allowed to either rise or fall, to move forward or backward, right or left. According to this myth, God took great alarm at this turn of events because the ant-men were incapable of adapting themselves to change. They no longer needed brains, so became brainless monsters of dependence. So He reduced their size to that of insects and began a new race of men.

The manner of operation of the social insects — the ants, the bees and the termites — has been the envy of dictators and would-be dictators; of many well intentioned reformers of varied hues. In the pattern of these insects is found their ideal of an "orderly and industrious" society of humans. Every aspiring dictator, both large and small, would like to ascend to the throne of "queen bee" of a world-wide human colony, in which every human would become subservient to the dictator's own wishes and would serve his plan with unwavering loyalty.

The social insects demonstrate a near approach to the ideal of the socialist society. What appears to be a devotion to duty among them cannot be denied. The members of the colony perform assigned tasks without question. Order and industry seem to prevail. The wishes of the individual insect are not allowed to come in conflict with his bounden duty to the colony. Unlimited cooperation, with a total lack of competition within their society, seems to prevail. In fact, the individual insect seems incapable of either a thought or a wish.

But other features should be noted about these insects, features that always accompany the ones so enticing to the dictator. It is impossible to have the one without the other. Even the queen bee, which they admire, is enslaved to biological duty rather than being free to carry out any personal wishes.

These insect colonies are highly materialistic. Moral and spiritual considerations play no part. They are coldly harsh in their purpose and performance. They are "inhuman" and wholly lacking in anything like the warmth of human love and compassion. Population is rigidly controlled. By killing those that do not work and by ruthlessly destroying the ill and the aged, full employment and "high" production is maintained — however high may be possible under this unprogressive design of life. A high "national income" is maintained by imposing compulsion of labor at an early age, by compulsion of long work weeks and by prohibiting vacations either with or without pay. Whereas the individual insect exhibits no self-interest, the selfish interests of the colony are substituted therefore; the two are in one sense similar, though the colony-selfishness operates on a huge scale whereby the mass of insects are driven into supporting it by blind allegiance. Not only is there a disciplinary violence of a cruel sort within the colony, but its members are forced to participate in violent wars with outsiders.

The devotion of individual insects to their assigned tasks is not, apparently, a work of love on behalf of a purpose embraced by conscious choice. Their diligence to duty is, instead, more like that of a locomotive which labors to haul a load. The engineer guiding their labors is the Unseen Hand of a biological control.

The characteristics of these insects have become nearly stable through untold ages of time. Their life task is somehow pre-determined, and the shackles of their destiny are firmly attached from the very beginning of each individual's life process. The individual insect is born into a system of slavery that leaves him with even less control over his own activity and destiny than is enjoyed by the caste-born baby in India. Their unwavering loyalty is, so far as we know, a blind loyalty rather than one of understanding and choice. The social-insect design of life allows none of the luxury of individual choice; it allows no liberty.

The human individual is quite unlike the social insect in some important respects. He is highly competitive with some of his fellow men, while being highly cooperative with others. He is motivated, not by the materialistic purpose alone, but by moral and spiritual purposes as well. Having the capacity for independent thought and action, he possesses the urge for liberty and the will to be free. He is designed to be the master of his own destiny, within the limits set by the natural law of universal forces. These qualities induce him to reject and rebel against any blind loyalty or subservience to any of his fellows or to any other form of life, because his moral and spiritual concepts obligate him to a Higher Order. He knows that he cannot serve two masters, which means that any earthly dictator who would be his god comes out no better than second in every race — second to his sense of personal responsibility to God and truth as he sees it. Thus the human seems to be cursed with a chronic itch to do something different from his fellows, to be always rebelling against something; we shall shortly see why.

Human rebellion takes many forms. It may be a small boy who decides to study piscatorial problems beside his favorite stream in the raw of nature, rather than to remain in the schoolroom where "compulsory learning" is administered by a hired teacher from an approved textbook. Or it may be a soldier who would break ranks to study a specimen of botany beside the road. Or it may be any one of innumerable other ways by which persons try their hands at some new task, or their minds at some new idea, or travel to view new sights. The recalcitrant human animal is the everlasting woe of the dictator, because he is constantly upsetting the dictator's personal plans and hopes.

Change results from the desire for improvement. The human wants liberty to try new things. He wants to get ahead and to improve his personal abilities. The opportunity to do so is the source of his happiness, and that is why liberty and the liberal design of social conduct are so essential to human happiness.

The human urge for liberty and the will to be free cannot be cast off by a simple vow or by any other similar means, because these qualities are fixed into his nature as firmly as is the loyalty of the bee to his colony. It would take a long period of biological change to fix into the human form of life the qualities found in the social insects, even if such a change were desired.

Human capacity for independent thought and action, when coupled with variation throughout the universe, is what gives rise to progress. And there is progress only to the extent that this capacity is allowed to operate under liberty. So next we shall consider, briefly, the nature of variation and its relation to progress under liberty.[2]

[2] In Appendix II is given some further explanation of the historical development and mathematical aspects of variation.

VARIATION SEEMS TO BE a universal law of nature. It seems to prevail everywhere and in the most minute detail. A person's fingerprint, for instance, serves to distinguish him from every other member of the human race.

Until a little over a century ago, variation was thought to have no pattern or purpose, and was considered to be an "accidental" and chaotic feature of nature. It defied all forms of scientific treatment, because it seemed to be totally unpredictable. Thus it was considered to be an evil, something to be prevented rather than being thought of as an inevitable force of nature with which to cooperate.

A little over a century ago the mathematical astronomers discovered, for the first time so far as we know, that there is an orderliness in variation as it occurs in nature. They found that variation appears to be disorderly and chaotic only because of a lack of arrangement, whereby its pattern is revealed. Once variation is placed in arrangement, these variations change from the ugliness of chaos into the beauty of an orderly pattern that is both interesting and predictable.

Admitting that a vast amount of scientific work is needed on this subject of variation, its present degree of development suggests that in it lies something of profound significance. If these concepts should finally become established as tenable, comparable to the law of falling bodies in physics, a person with any spiritual faith whatsoever is forced to conclude that variation is one of the "laws of nature"; that variation exists according to plan, and with a purpose of a High Order; that it has existed all along in spite of the ignorance that has prevailed about it.

When one comes face to face with the vastness of this subject of variation, and its possible import, a sense of humility emerges that all but silences him on the subject forever. Yet its possible importance and relation to the matter of liberty leads one to risk speculating about its design and purpose in the order of things. But in doing so, tolerance is requested toward probable errors in exploratory thought.

"Variety is the spice of life."

Variation appears everywhere, and in one or another definite pattern of form. And so a purpose in variation must be assumed. What is its purpose?[3]

Variation is the source of change, and its only source. As a result of variation it is possible for "offspring" to differ from their "parents," whether the process be that of reproduction of life or its counterpart in non-life such as the formation of compounds in chemistry. Without variation, no such changes could occur.

Change is, in turn, the source of "progress." Progress, briefly, is a change in belief, concept or their applications into "devices" which stand up under the tests of time and experience so as to have increasing acceptance among free people. In a word, it is an expansion of truth, or applied truth as tested by the only means at our disposal.

Not all change is what we call progress; change may be either progress or retrogression.[4] But progress is not possible unless there is change, which in turn is not possible unless there is variation.

In short, the opportunity for progress appears to be the purpose of variation.

Variation also affords relief from unbelievable — even incomprehensible — monotony. It is, therefore, a source of enjoyment for humans, which is made possible by their intelligence and capacity for discrimination.

A world without variation would be a strange world indeed. How could there be beauty? How could there be love? Courtship,

[3] Some of the more technical aspects of this question are given in Appendix III.

[4] The matter of distinguishing between what is favorable and what is unfavorable is discussed in Appendix IV.

at least, would be a strange process quite lacking in verve if all the eligible candidates were exactly alike. How could there be any purpose in going to the circus, or to the ball game, or engaging in any sport or competitive enterprise whatsoever, if all the animals and all the human players were exactly alike? From whence would come any enjoyment, if the monotony of ever-the-same were to be always present? A day of living in such a world would certainly lead a person to visualize heaven as a place where variation is rampant.

CHAPTER NINE

THE UNCOMMON MAN

VARIATION, AS WE HAVE SEEN, results in progress when the changes are favorable ones. If favorable changes are to be made, they must be the result of free choice. Otherwise unfavorable changes and regression will be the result.

Free choice means liberty.

Thus it is concluded that variation offers the seeds of progress because it is the origin of change; that change will take the form of progress when, and to whatever extent, liberty allows these seeds to bloom into favorable changes.

The capacity for independent decisions and free choice is the precious attribute of humans that makes progress possible. The social insects apparently lack this capacity. That is why, under liberty, it is possible for humans to capitalize on the opportunities arising from the variations that abound in nature in a manner that the social insects cannot.

The analogy of growing a crop may illustrate the contributing forces that lead to progress. Variation is the seed of progress. Liberty is the soil and the climate in which the seed will sprout and grow. Human capacity for independent decisions and free choice is the husbandman who nurtures the crop during the period of its growth and harvest.

The capacity for free choice and intelligent action is a precious and perishable thing, to be nurtured and guarded with care. Rocks do not have this capacity for independent, intelligent action. Nearly all forms of life lack it. The social insects, if they ever had it, seem to have lost it long ago. When unused, it will apparently atrophy in the manner of muscles that are inactive. Without liberty the brain becomes imprisoned as though behind iron doors; thoughts and initiative die.

The capacity for free choice and intelligent action may also become lost in any species of life by the process of adverse selection. Presumably this is what happened to the social insects in their early history, in the manner implied in the Russian fable. In like manner the capacity for progress could become lost in the human race; the firing squad of an authoritarian nation brings this about quickly and vividly.

VARIATION, and the human capacity to compound progress out of this variation under liberty, is the foundation of progress.

Human ability is highly variable. Presumably it follows the law of variation described by the harmonic series.[1] Human abilities are spread over a wide range so that very few persons are on the upside, and the number increases with a downward movement along the scale of ability into mediocrity. The "common man" is well named because there are so many of us. And the "uncommon man" is the one who has developed and put to use his extremely rare abilities.

The person is rare indeed who is capable of the basic discoveries on which progress is built. Among such persons have been Aristotle, Leonardo da Vinci, Beethoven, Pasteur, and Edison, to name a few among the distinctive ones whose accomplishments grew out of this variation among mankind.

[1] This pattern of variation is described in Appendix II.

But the mere existence of variation is not enough to generate progress. Rocks are highly variable, too, for instance, but something is lacking and they cannot generate progress. Nor can the social insects generate progress. If there is to be progress, variation must be accompanied by the capacity for independent thought and action, the capacity for choice, careful preparation so as to make use of accumulated knowledge, and the willingness and opporunity to proceed alone in the search for truth. Man has these qualities in varying degrees, but only a few persons have all the necessary qualities in the combination required for important contributions to progress. It is to these few that essentially all progress is due.

Extreme glorification of the common man may be popular, but it involves a serious threat to an understanding of the essentials of progress. It feeds the evil of vainglory, dangerously.

A great deal of credit is, of course, due each person who performs as best he can the task he has tackled, using the abilities with which he has been endowed by nature. Most of the activity in the world is that of the seemingly menial tasks necessary for life and happiness to which we have become accustomed; but the performance of all these worthy tasks is not the progress of which we are speaking.

A person with x ability who performs an x sized task with x perfection deserves as much personal credit as one with $100x$ ability who performs a $100x$ sized task with $100x$ perfection; and he deserves more credit if the latter person should deliver to the extent of only $50x$, or half his capacity.

In appraising a person, it is what he does with what he has that counts. In appraising the requirements of progress, we are unconcerned with personal glories and it is what is delivered that counts.

Contrary to general impression, the path to greatness is as

difficult as it is rare. It is not a rosy path of ease. It is a path strewn with hazards and failures. Just as most mutations are self-destructive, most attempts to discover new truths and to peer into the unknown yield either illusion or failure. The mutant dies of its inborn deficiencies; most pioneering of thought or action ends in failure, and at best one can expect to fail time and time again before any final success.

Not alone that, but the uncommonly great person is generally misunderstood. That is the expected result of being uncommon. Both the genius and the idiotic dunce are "peculiar" persons, misunderstood by the large number of us who cannot really understand either of them. One cannot exceed his own limited capacities to understand which is which, as between the two ends of an array of human abilities.

Most contributors to progress have been treated with either indifference, scorn or derision in their time. Pasteur was forced to endure the greatest of intellectual indignities when first he pronounced his discoveries.

The pioneer of progress most likely will be a lonely and persecuted soul, who must learn to find his reward elsewhere than in the concurrent appreciations of his contemporaries. As Professor John R. Baker has explained, the pioneer of discovery and progress is one with an independent spirit who will tolerate no master; he will bear privation and starvation, if necessary, rather than to surrender to another his rights in the pursuit of truth.[2]

Only in history are his accomplishments likely to be recognized as noteworthy. To do his work, and to contribute to progress, he must unavoidably be different, act differently and think differently from his fellow men; if it were not so, his works would not constitute discovery and progress. He finds his satisfaction in the

---

[2] John R. Baker, *Science and the Planned State* (New York: The Macmillan Company, 1945).

discovery of truth as a discovery, not in the personal glory involved; in being right rather than in being popular. He must expect persecution of a sort from many persons, and perhaps even from the "authorities" in the field of his discovery, as Pasteur experienced.

The pioneer of progress is one who believes truth to be something different from the beliefs that prevail around him. There is not much chance for progress when these persons are prohibited from practicing honesty in the expression of their rare beliefs. In requesting the privileges of liberty, he is merely asking for the privilege of practicing honesty in the search for and expression of his beliefs.

He should, of course, be willing to grant the same right to others as that which he requests for himself, and to be tolerant of disagreements. A person of rare beliefs — including the genius of progress — in many instances has so little understanding of liberty and such an intense devotion to his own unpopular beliefs that he tries to impose his personal beliefs on others by intellectual authoritarianism, and tries to grasp the power required for the attempt. That may be the reason why so many renowned pioneers in various fields of knowledge become addicts of a controlled economy, and contribute to the destruction of liberty which is so essential to their own work. This was noticeable in Hitler's Germany. It is noticeable in our own country, in our day, and has become a serious threat to liberty.

THE RACE FOR DISCOVERY and progress in society is a peculiar sort of race. The actual winner seems to lose and the losers win. As we have seen, the winner of discovery must often endure scorn and other forms of indignity from others who assume that the poor soul is suffering from dangerous hallucinations. Yet the benefits of discovery and progress go largely to those who lost in the race of discovery, and who have even scorned the winner.

It is unavoidable that they shall come to consume most of the fruits of discovery and progress.

The "common man," who has lost the race of making the actual discovery, reaps the harvest of the seeds that he has scorned. It takes little ability to press a light switch, after the rare developments of a Franklin and an Edison have thus mastered and simplified its uses. The world has to wait a long, long time for a Ford or a Kettering, but most anyone can learn to drive a car. The capacity to consume is common, not rare, and most of us are capable of consuming what only the uncommon man is capable of discovering and producing.

The pioneers of progress, as distinct from those who process and use the fruits of progress, derive little direct benefit from their own work. Pasteur consumed little of the vaccines that have been made as a result of his discoveries; he had only one life to lose from disease, but these discoveries are saving innumerable other lives. An automobile inventor drives few of the cars resulting from his invention. Beethoven consumed little of the enjoyment that has resulted from his talents. Those who stood on the shores and derided "Fulton's Folly" were among the multitudes who later rode on such craft. And among the crowds at the ticket windows of airline offices have been those who jeered at the "foolish notions" of the Wright brothers; little ability is required to climb aboard a plane that is to fly from New York to Bombay. None of these pioneers of progress gained much wealth from their work of discovery, which so many others enjoy.

In this age of political glorification of the common man, of mediocrity, and of the masses and the opinions of the masses, it must not be forgotten that if there had been only common men down through the ages we would still be living as savages. Except for the progress that stems from the uncommon man, ours would still be an existence like that of the lowest animals.

An excellent expression of this idea appeared in an interpretation of Toynbee's *Study of History*:[3]

It will be seen that Toynbee's is a great-man theory: "human individuals and not human societies . . . make history." In a growing Civilization the creative leaders lead "the uncreative mass" by enlisting the faculty of *mimesis*; in many subtle ways the mass of people "imitate" the Creative Minority so that the whole body social is able to grow *en masse* and in harmony. In a dying Civilization the Creative Minority is displaced by the Dominant Minority, and repression is substituted for *mimesis*. The mimetic song of Orpheus, who leads his people into the light of Civilization, is drowned out by "the raucous shouts of the drill-sergeant," who herds them back into the darkness.

Progress will be slowed to whatever extent the demands of the common man are allowed to rob the uncomman man of the opportunity to generate progress. Liberty affords him this opportunity to use his talents, and nothing else does. Discovery and progress cannot be forced; at best they can only be allowed to occur.

Most discovery results from a seemingly accidental hybridization of ideas, in a like manner as strains of corn are crossed to produce the rarely outstanding hybrid. Perhaps this is why basic discovery so often occurs in unsuspected places, by unsuspected persons whose rare powers of observation and comprehension have permitted them to grasp the significance of something that occurred within their scope of vision or experience, for which they may not even have been searching. Perhaps this is why rigid over-specialization and restriction in the search for new discoveries so often ends in failure to attain the objective; the narrow confines of the search prevents a hybridization of ideas from which progress so often springs. The new things of progress are often found by those who "know nothing about the subject."

Such is the story of why variation contains the seeds of progress. That is why the fruits of progress will be born only in the

[3] Richard Chase, "Toynbee: The Historian as Artist," *The American Scholar,* Summer, 1947, p. 275.

environment of liberty, where free play on the scale of variations can generate discovery and progress. That is why the destruction of all liberty would stop all progress, and set in motion the forces of retrogression.

Only under liberty can discovery and the origin of progress rear its lonely head, in some wholly unpredictable time, place and form, by some "unknown" person. Progress cannot be plotted and blueprinted in advance; that is why it is progress. Only in retrospect can discovery be identified.

If the planner could plan discovery for others, he probably would have made the discovery himself in the first place. If he is more able in this respect than the others, he is wasting his time not to do it himself; if he is less able, he can hardly plan it for others who are more able than he is. The notion that a blueprint for discovery can be drawn in advance is to assert that the planner somehow has the power to scrutinize the inscrutable, or fathom the unfathomable. It is not an act of discovery for a planner to buy the discoverer's groceries or clean his tools, or to be the nominal head of the political bureau which pays his salary.

Much false credit is given to planning for "accomplishments" that would have taken place anyhow. One is reminded of the story of the fly on the chariot wheel which thought that he was the source of the power that propelled the vehicle. A governmental agency empowered to plan the size of the potato crop, for instance, is likely to change its "plans" after learning that farmers' intentions to plant are at variance with their plan as previously announced. It is hardly respectful for a planning agency to have its plans proved "ineffective" (a wrong prediction of what farmers would do in spite of the plan). If a person should become empowered of "planning" the migration of the birds, it would be helpful for him to have some factual information on which to base his plans; he could then plan to have the birds go toward the equator in the fall and back toward the poles in the spring.

Truth, when newly born, is always an ugly stranger amidst the untruth and superstition of its time; it cannot live except as it is allowed the protection of liberty, which serves to protect newly-discovered truth in the same way as a mother protects the new-born child. For the seedlings of progress, like the more advanced forms of life, are unable at birth to care for themselves. They will die in infancy except for careful protection.

CHAPTER TEN

GOVERNMENT AND PROGRESS

GOVERNMENT, as previously discussed, is a repressive force. Within its scope, it prescribes patterns of conduct whereby the citizens are forbidden from doing certain things. Every deviation from these decrees is judged to be "lawlessness," punishable even unto death.

The first recorded laws under government, for instance, were those of 3800 years ago which decreed that any market transaction other than at a specified price was unlawful. This, within its scope, was an attempt to eliminate all variation.

In the acts of government, a singleness of conduct is attempted which by its very nature defies the law of variation. Every violation of a decree is officially judged to be an evil. The exercise of human capacity for independent judgment, free choice and action is curbed by government. This is in violation of liberty, the requisite of progress.

As previously discussed, however, certain governmental activity increases the scope of liberty throughout society. The repression of certain actions of persons that are in violation of the rules of a liberal society results in a net increase in liberty. Up to that point government can generate progress, but when it goes beyond that point in enforcing a singleness of conduct it destroys liberty and progress in that society.

The result of an expansion of governmental action beyond that defined as the objective of government in a liberal society is to make human conduct more and more similar to that of the social insects — involuntary servitude to the unknown. These insects offer an illustration of what happens when variation is considered to be a thing of enmity, and steps are taken to reduce it more and more in scope. Thus, over the ages, these insects have developed into their present form.

In the attainment of a fixed purpose and socialistic design of the insect colony, any individual insect that exhibited any capacity for thought and free choice presumably had to be destroyed in a continuous purge. If one of them should evidence individuality or dissimilarity from the pattern of conduct prescribed in The Plan, he was an enemy of that society. He was a traitor and met the fate of a traitor. The question was not whether he was right or wrong.

This ruthless purge of all dissenters from the "pattern of conduct in harmony with an orderly society" left only those insects having a minimum capacity for thought and independent action. It left only a living counterpart of the fixed qualities of chemical elements in a stone or a brick. As a consequence, variation, so far as it relates to the matter of intelligence, the urge for liberty, and the will to be free in making decisions of choice, was bred out of these strains of life. So we now find among these insects a high degree of standardization of these particular qualities. Theirs is an unintelligent conformity to an unprogressive society. Their lack of progress is the unavoidable consequence of a bounden duty to a predestined role. The same will happen to humans, if they should ever bow in bounden duty to the wishes of a dictator over a period of time.

Carried to the ultimate in eliminating variation and its manifestations, a completely authoritarian government becomes the result. Such a government would declare all progress to be illegal. This would, of course, be unintentional. But the fact remains that the extreme egotist is a natural dictator, one who would control others with the intent of preventing them from making "mistakes"; and he deems himself to be the only one worthy of judgment in the matter of what is and what is not a mistake.

In response to these observations, one may inquire why a government that acts in harmony with variation and change could not become an agency of progress. This would mean allowing the individual to follow his wisdom and conscience without prohibition or penalty, provided he does not trespass on the rights of others under the concepts of liberalism. But why would it be necessary for government to decree that a person shall do as he will? That is precisely the type of thing that does not require an enactment of government. A policeman would not be very busy making people do what they want to do!

For government to act in such a manner is not to govern at all. Thus to argue for governmental permission of variation and change is to argue for an absence of government. The small boy, in similar vein, was said to have asked his "ultra-progressive" teacher if he had to do what he wanted to do.

For government to issue permits for the rule of variation is a rather questionable claim to authority. If variation is a universal law, governmental bodies need not notify the Maker of His rights in guiding the affairs of the universe, nor can they without false authority issue any such decrees to the citizens. The truth of the matter is that these governments do not wish to grant rights of variation. It is not surprising that an authoritarian government declares the laws of inheritance and of variation to be not to their liking, and attempts to make both religious belief and inheritance of variable characteristics non-existent by mere edict.

A government cannot rescind universal laws by enacting contrary statutory laws or administrative decrees. When this is attempted, failure to comply with the law or decree is certain to follow. Citizens are placed in a most undignified position; they must choose between being a criminal in the eyes of the law or a sinner in the eyes of the Maker. A problem that perplexes many religious persons and scientists, who have knowledge of these natural laws, is that of identifying the point in this contradiction of authority where rebellion is justified against the would-be usurpation of Divine authority.

IT IS COMMONLY BELIEVED that the "democratic process" will assure progress. But there is no way of designing excessive governmental activity so as to assure that it will aid progress rather than stop progress.

Progress arises in every instance out of an extreme minority of opinion, not the majority of opinion. The seedlings of progress are often so small and unnoticed that they are ignored by those who would otherwise destroy them in ignorance as "evil" thought or acts. But if everything were to be subjected to majority rule, every step of progress would presumably be destroyed in its infancy.

When we consider the separate historic events that comprise what we now accept as the steps of progress, and if we note how unacceptable they were in their early day, it should be clear that little progress could have occurred under a rule of the majority over the ages. As illustration, the potato, a marvelously productive new crop from South America, was barred from introduction into the agriculture of England during the extended time when this type of rule by the members of each community was in operation; it barred individual freedom of decision and action, and prevented the progress that always arises because someone is willing to hazard the trying of something new.

Neither does the device of compromise prevent the acts of government from stopping progress. Truth is not a thing that can be compromised. A thing is right or it is wrong. Principle cannot be compromised; it can only be abandoned. The route to the discovery of truth is to allow a person to be wholly right or wholly wrong. Compromise is bound to be wrong. The search for truth is impeded by the fact that a person who thus abandons reason and who adopts the compromise means of always being wrong is so commonly termed a reasonable person, and crowned with virtue and perhaps given a position of power!

Ignorance and false beliefs, the barriers to truth and progress, are harbored by the majority of persons about all things except the core of "accepted truth." Their numbers make them the rulers in the democratic process. They should not be empowered with rule over the "creative minority" at the crucial time when these steps of progress are being taken and an acceptance of newly discovered truth is being slowly gained.

An essential feature of a liberal government is the protection of minorities, and of the rights of minorities against plunder by the majority. The ultimate of minorities is one person. And so the ultimate of liberalism, as it has been defined herein, is the protection of each person against the plunder of one or more other persons. This makes it possible for one person to be protected while he sows the seeds of progress, by withdrawing from the stampede of unreason that is around him. He must be protected, else there can be no progress. The protection must be general, covering all persons equally, because there can be no way to know in advance who is the person who will make the contribution to progress.

Progress always hangs by a slender thread, which can easily become severed. That is why progress has been so slow and uncommon over the history of the human race.

Progress is but a step away from retrogression. And whereas progress is a difficult upward climb, the slide down the slope of retrogression is so simple that even the most ignorant can negotiate it. A dictator who is totally incapable of any contribution to progress is likely to be skilled in its destruction.

Retrogression, once started, tends to accelerate. That is why in the past the slow advancement of various "civilizations" have quickly dissolved into "dark ages." The slow and painful gains of centuries, whereby progress under liberty is built upon the accumulated experience of the ages and wisdom of the sages, can become lost in a short space of time. The same stroke that destroys liberty and the chance for progress creates a power which releases the tides of unreason, under a false prophet who forces wholesale adherence to untruth among those within his domain.

The many users of the benefits of progress, especially in a democracy, hold in their hands the tools for the destruction of the fruits of progress. When once they have destroyed the liberty on which progress feeds and grows, they will have bequeathed to their children and to their children's children — to generation on generation that is to follow — an age of poverty and of social disintegration. That is our present threat.

Variation must be respected and protected, since it is the source of progress. To impose punishment on all that is at variance is to poison all progress. Nature's law of variation deserves full sway over wide scope, and it is improper for government to intercede except where one person trespasses on the rights of another under liberty.

CHAPTER ELEVEN

LIBERTY AND PEACE

THE TIME MAY HAVE COME when we can again search more freely for the root-cause of peace without being met automatically with charges of being a "pacifist." If pacifist means embracing the objective of peace, it should be no disgrace to be a pacifist.

Unfortunately, there are those who find in war and deadly conflict a form of amusement suited to their tastes. These remarks are offered to those who are in search of a maximum of peace, by honorable means, in the hope that they may find stimulation in that search.

CONFLICT, whether in its larger form of "war" or in one of its lesser forms, will exist increasingly as liberty is curbed.

This assertion is offered as a hypothesis. If it be correct, it means that the route to peace is to increase liberty among individuals throughout the world; and there is no other means. If it be correct, any combination of force by whatever means and under whatever excuse will generate conflict in one or another of its forms, and will most likely end in the worst form of all — war.

War, banditry, mutiny, insurrection, riot, rebellion and murder are all forms of conflict differing in size. The various forms of conflict may also differ in other respects, not here of concern. Some conflicters may wear uniforms whereas others wear more conventional clothes. Some conflicters may wear official badges or insignia, some may receive medals for proficiency in conflict, and others may be given handcuffs for having participated — if caught by the right persons. Some may be elevated in office and in esteem because of their participation, whereas others may be demoted and disgraced. It all depends on the nature and form of the conflict; on whether or not it has been legalized; on whether both participants are within one nation or not; and on other differences. But all forms of conflict describe the absence of peace, and if the objective is to have a maximum of peace, there must be a minimum of conflict in any of its forms.

Conflict is a major occupation in the affairs of the world. One study reports that one form — war — has engaged the major countries of Europe for about half the time since the year 1500.[1]

Another study gives an estimate of 59 million persons who have died because of conflict in all its forms during the last century and a quarter.[2] About four-fifths of this total number died as a direct result of the larger wars, which is the major cause of death in conflict, even though wars are few in number. Murders and the other lesser forms of conflict, though highly numerous, have accounted for only about one-fourth of one per cent of all the deaths from all causes in the world during this period.

These figures suggest the importance to peace of preventing the processes whereby conflict amasses into the larger affairs. Much better, perhaps, would be to endure the greater frequency of small conflict rather than to suffer the consequences of less frequent but more devastating major conflicts, if conflict in some

[1] Q. Wright, A Study of War (Chicago: University of Chicago Press, 1942).

[2] Lewis F. Richardson, "Variation of the Frequency of Fatal Quarrels with Magnitude," Journal of the American Statistical Association, Dec., 1948.

form is unavoidable and if even the smaller ones must be endured as safety valves.

Many persons can be induced to fight some distant "enemy" they do not know, over some issue they do not understand, while in the abundant company of kinsmen who likewise do not know what the grandiose affair is all about. People are much less inclined to engage in conflict with an "enemy" who is their next-door neighbor, where the issue is clear to both parties; this form of dispute is much more likely to be settled out of conflict, peacefully.

Government is the official manager of every major conflict. This is a strange situation when viewed purely from the aspect of conflict. It seems strange that a government compels the citizens to participate in large-scale conflict, but punishes them for engaging in certain minor forms of conflict.

The conduct of all the activities of government is of the nature of conflict if, as Richardson defines it, conflict means "malice aforethought." This is because government is engaged in enacting laws and punishing the violators; it engages in processes of force and compels support of all its operations by the citizens. It is engaged in repression, and imposes processes of force on those who come under its edicts. The voluntary acts of persons do not involve conflict, and do not require the enactment of government in order to be performed.

So war means conflict built on conflict and is, in a sense, conflict pyramiding itself. Perhaps that is why war is, by all odds, the most serious form of conflict.

It is no coincidence that large-scale wars are the product of dictatorships, or of the acts of aspiring dictators. In its earlier stages of growth, the dictator's grasp for more power results mainly in internal conflict. Later it bursts its seams and becomes external conflict. Government of the scope and design of a liberal government, as previously defined, would seem to be engaged in an unavoidable degree of conflict; and so, to that extent it serves as an agency for maximizing liberty and minimizing conflict. But when government expands beyond that size and scope, where a maximum of liberty exists in society, the total of conflict is thereby increased.

THE HYPOTHESIS has been given that conflict will exist increasingly as liberty is curbed. Or, conflict is the result of the loss of liberty.

Stated another way, liberty and peace are to one another as cause and effect. Is this true?

If liberty were complete, and if a person restricted himself to what is properly his concern, how could there be conflict except perhaps as a pantomime for purposes of amusement? What would there be to fight about if liberty were universal?

Violation of liberty, and nothing else, is the basic cause of conflict. The violation of liberty may affect either the person or his property; it may be in the form of either a loss of liberty or the threat of a loss, real or imagined. Under any of these conditions, man's will to be free impels him to strike at that force which is infringing on his liberty or threatening to do so.

The initiative of joining conflict may be taken by one who, in the act of "aggression," attempts to take liberty away from others; Genghis Khan and those who captured slaves in Africa were both of this type. Or the conflict may occur in the process of regaining lost liberty through "rebellion," against the yoke of already-lost liberties; the French and American Revolutions were of this type. Or the conflict may be an "offensive defense," designed to strike at the assumed future aggressor first, before he strikes; this is aggression despite any attempt at rationalization of it as being "wise strategy"; the presumed intent of the "enemy" can never be proved in advance of his act of aggression; many national conflicts fall in this class, and it is to be noted that most of the wars of history were "defensive" wars, as written into each country's own records of history. Conflict in all its sizes and forms, not just wars, originates in one or another of these settings of lost liberty.

The real crime against liberty does not, as we have seen, always occur at the time when the conflict started, because the conflict may be a rebellion against a loss of liberty at a much earlier time. The actual conflict in such instances is started by the oppressed in order to regain his previously-lost liberty. They are rebellions against the yoke of unbearable and illiberal power. Such was the setting of Patrick Henry's famous words in 1775:

> Is life so dear or peace so sweet as to be purchased at the price of chains and slavery? Forbid it, Almighty God! I know not what course others may take; but as for me, give me liberty, or give me death!

One may question, however, whether the lost liberty of chains and slavery, or the encroachment of unwanted power in any of its forms, is fairly to be termed peace.

The original loss of liberty leading to rebellion has been, in most instances, accomplished by the oppressor through seemingly peaceful and lawful means; Edmund Burke said that it occurs "under some delusion." The victims in these instances, because of either ignorance or "tolerance," had allowed their rights under liberty to erode until finally, in a panic of realization, violent rebellion breaks out in the hope of regaining the lost liberty. The basic cause — liberty lost in an earlier day — tends to become obscured by the furor of the conflict.

"Meeting power with power" and "balance of power" are concepts with wide appeal in international affairs. Threats of force are used as the excuse for enlarging a counter-force, and vice versa until the inevitable conflict is abandoned because of sheer exhaustion rather than from settlement of its underlying causes.

The same argument thus used in international affairs has also been used in "industrial warfare." It is argued that the power of unions must be increased to meet the threatening power of business, or that the power of business must be increased to meet the threatening power of the unions, or that the power of government must be built up to meet the threat of one or both of these.

The basis for this method of meeting a threat to peace probably is the notion that size and might are synonymous. It is the belief that an increase in size means proportionately greater concentration of power, which becomes might in proportion to its increase in size. This belief then leads directly to greater and greater concentrations of authority for "defensive purposes." Concentration of authority means loss of liberty without fail, because authority cannot reside in two places at the same time. Completing the circle, then, leads one to the questionable conclusion that peace is to be found in the abandonment of liberty. Any such conclusion is confronted with the conflicting evidence of Hitler and Mussolini, and of many others throughout history.

The belief that size and might are synonymous sounds plausible until one ponders certain questions. Why does large size so often meet defeat at the hands of that which is lesser in size? Why did dinosaurs become extinct under competition with lesser forms of life, rather than to grow ever larger and larger over the ages? And "trees do not grow to the sky." Why can microbes kill forms of life impressively larger than they are, without entering into any authoritarian combine with that as its express purpose? Why have all the great aggregations of power of the famous conquerors of history fallen of their own weight to an opposition that derives its strength from something other than mere size? Why was Gandhi's passive resistance and Christ's method of "attack" so effective? We cannot deny that a form of might resides in size, but size is not might per se. There appears to be some form of inherent weakness in size and aggregations of power, which tends to cause their downfall.

Perhaps the problem of peace should be approached from a new and unconventional direction.[8] On the record, at least, the solution would seem to lie elsewhere than in the methods that have been tried again and again without even a semblance of success. What is more, the customary means of trying to remove a difficulty by the use of force and power seems always to demoralize those who adopt it; observing this may have suggested to Bentham his definition of war, as "mischief on the largest scale." It may explain why human reason seems to go on furlough, for the duration of serious conflict and in many instances thereafter. It may explain why both sides of most wars seem to come out as losers.

Perhaps the only route to peace is to increase liberty by breaking up each and every source and form of power, to the greatest possible extent and by peaceful means prior to its inevitable eruption into conflict. There must be substituted for the conflict of power a code of justice whereby the enemy of liberty becomes, not certain persons or certain nations in their entirety, but only those acts of any person or of any nation which violate the liberal design of society. Once this concept has been grasped, the words of Thomas Paine, when he said that one who would make his own liberty secure must guard even his own enemy from oppression, comes to have a new beauty of meaning. The futility of wholesale conflict as a defense of liberty then becomes clear.

Personalizing the enemy of liberty makes it impossible to come to grips with the true enemy, which is an act of the person. One act of a person may be in violation of liberty, and that is the enemy; all the other acts of that person may be in harmony with

[8] See: Chang Hsin-hai, "The Moral Basis of World Peace," *The Annals*, Vol. 258 (July, 1948), 79-89.

liberty. To personalize the enemy of liberty in this way is as though a surgeon, who has been engaged to cope with a malignant growth, were to personalize his enemy and kill the patient as his professional duty; if this procedure be wrong in surgery, can it be right in civil and international affairs?

In like manner, we are prone to personalize and nationalize the enemy of liberty, so that in the ensuing war the object becomes that of trying to kill the patient — those who are lovers of liberty within that nation as well as those who are violators of liberty, all of whom have been conscripted into the enemy's armed forces indiscriminately.

This line of thought offers no panacea to a quick certainty of world peace. But to whatever extent this analysis is correct, there is no panacea or shortcut to peace. If the object be peace, how can it be attained by the use of force in attacking, indiscriminately, that which is liberty along with that which is not?

When we consider the deep-seated desire of persons for liberty, and when we note the relationship between liberty and peace, could wars occur except as the power to drive a whole nation into war comes to be vested in the hands of one or a few persons — perhaps even someone in a foreign "friendly nation"? That person may have motives entirely different from the persons they are presumed to be serving. He may be overmindful of the personal glories of war.

History reports in glowing terms of the glories of war and of victory. Emblazoned on the pages of history are the names of those who happened to have been the political leaders during the pageantry and historic din of sacrificial conflict. But in many instances those who thus acquire historic recognition are merely engaged in reaping the bitter consequences of their own past mistakes, which caused the destruction of the underpinnings of liberty so that conflict resulted.

Largely unsung and unrecorded are the truly great whose wise and timely acts stopped the makings of the aggression at their source, and who in this way prevented major wars. Their greatness, we may trust, is safely recorded in more important places and in a manner more substantial than mere popularity and common renown, more permanently than statue and shrine, in forms where human errors of judgment cannot tarnish or pollute the greatness. The most deserving glories of peace are to be found in the calm of battles not fought, and in the personages of those who prevented them from being fought.

PART 2

ON MEASURING LIBERTY

Abstract liberty, like other mere abstractions, is not
to be found.

EDMUND BURKE

CHAPTER TWELVE

A MEASURE OF LIBERTY

LIBERTY IS MORE than a word. It is a thing of substance that can be either present or absent, gained or lost. A person may be free or he may be a slave; presumably it is possible for that person to tell which is which, and that gives rise to the possibility of measurement.

We are concerned with the present status of liberty. If its status is to be discussed with accuracy, some specific measurements closely related thereto would be helpful. Otherwise the subject must endure futile debate in vague and meaningless terms. A means of measuring an important area where liberty is at stake will shortly be explained and applied to the United States.

This measure is not offered as a perfect measure of liberty, nor as a final answer to that question.[1] But even a rough measure may help to pave the way for a better one.

Strictly speaking, liberty itself defies measurement because it is basically a subjective matter with each person. Measurement is limited to the reflections of liberty, or the indirect evidences of its presence or absence. It is in that sense that the measurement of liberty will be discussed.

[1] Some of its limitations are given in Appendix V.

Failure to be able to come to direct grips with a thing should not completely discredit an attempt to measure it, however. Much of the work of science with which we are familiar and which we use as a guide to our beliefs and acts employs methods of indirection for gaining evidence about the thing being studied; indications of the thing are accepted in lieu of the thing itself, and are deemed to be evidence worthy of use. Illustrations include original work in astronomy, in the germ theory of disease, and in many parts of chemistry such as the development of the atomic table.

Liberty is divisible. It may be present or absent in different aspects of our daily lives, leaving a person partly free and partly slave. Each person may at any time be anywhere between 0 per cent and 100 per cent at liberty, or between 100 per cent and 0 per cent a slave.

If one were to speak of the status of liberty in an entire country like the United States, it would be necessary to represent it by an average for the liberties of all the persons in that country. This would make it possible to speak of liberty in a nation as being at some point between 0 per cent and 100 per cent, the same as for one person; it would offer a device by which to judge whether liberty in a nation has been increasing or decreasing over a period of time. Such a treatment on a national basis obscures, but it does not deny, that liberty is an individual matter; that liberty for any one of these persons may be either above or below the national average.

A simple fact, but one significant to interpreting the status of liberty on a national basis, is that one person has a maximum of 100 per cent liberty. If each of two persons enjoyed full liberty, with neither of them desiring to enslave the other, their average would be 100 per cent liberty $\left(\frac{100 + 100}{2}\right)$. If one of them acquired the desire to enslave the other, and did so, his liberty would still be only 100 per cent; that of his enslaved fellow would fall to 0 per cent, however, and their average liberty would fall to 50 per cent $\left(\dfrac{100 + 0}{2}\right)$.

A dictator over a hundred million persons has no more liberty (100 per cent) than if he desired not to be a dictator and was a free man among a hundred million free men. But the national average of liberty under the dictatorship would be near 0 per cent $\left(\dfrac{100 + 0 + 0 + 0\ldots.}{100,000,000}\right)$, whereas without the dictatorship it could be near 100 per cent.

The desire to enslave his fellows, on the part of one dictatorially inclined, means that his liberty cannot be as much as 100 per cent except as he is able to accomplish that feat. In being prevented from enslaving his fellows, he is deprived of a full measure of his liberty, as we have defined it; we might assume, as illustration in one instance, that its prevention meant a loss of half of that person's liberty, or of his willful desires. If he were the only one in the nation blighted with this illiberal desire, to allow him to grasp full power would reduce the average level of liberty for that nation to near zero $\left(\dfrac{100 + 0 + 0 + 0\ldots.}{100,000,000}\right)$; whereas curbing his grasp for power would allow liberty to be near 100 per cent in that nation $\left(\dfrac{50 + 100 + 100 + 100\ldots.}{100,000,000}\right)$.

These simple numerical representations serve to indicate how the national average of liberty is affected directly in proportion as there is enslavement by any means whatsoever, within a nation.

THE FOUNDATION of economic liberty has been defined as the right of a person to the product of his own labor. If this definition be accepted, it becomes a means by which to measure one's economic liberty — or its complement, the degree of economic slavery he is being forced to endure.

The slave is compelled to work for his master without any rights whatsoever to income that he may spend as he chooses. Nor does he have any rights to private property. Whatever economic living may be granted to the slave by his master is given to him in the same manner as one makes a gift to another, because there is no definite obligation involved; the slave has no right to demand any "pay" of food or other things; he has no means by which to assure himself of something to eat tomorrow, either from the work he does or from what he has saved. The master, of course, normally does not allow his slave to starve; he gives him food and necessities so that he may live to toil another day.

It may seem strange that the slave, totally lacking in liberty, frequently feels no strong resentment toward the master who has enslaved him. In fact, the slave may even feel grateful toward his master who "so kindly gives me food and necessities with which to live, and without which I would surely die." It is said that many a newly-freed slave after the War Between the States feared liberty because, due to the narrow vision of his experience as a slave, he acquired this strange feeling of kindness toward his oppressor. A similar feeling is reported to have been held by the oppressed in Hitler's Germany, and in Stalin's Russia; and we have noted the same feeling among those who have acquired the habit of leaning on a benevolent government in our own country. All these victims of a lost liberty are unmindful of the fruits of liberty, due to the blindness which compulsory or voluntary slavery has caused. "Forgive them, for they know not. . . .", but let them become free so that they may know!

If a slaveholder grants to his slave a daily wage of $10 — the market equivalent of what the slave produces — and then, after paying it, takes it all back again, one could hardly claim that the slave had thereby gained his economic liberty. The slave might properly say to his master: "You may as well keep my pay in the first place. I have no economic liberty unless I can keep it and can have free choice in its spending."

Suppose that the master, instead of taking back all of the $10, should take back only three-fourths, or one-half, or one-fourth of it. Would it then be correct to say that the slave lacked economic liberty to the extent of three-fourths, or one-half, or one-fourth, as the case might be? According to our definition of economic liberty, this suggests a rough measure of the degree of economic liberty he is then enjoying, even though he is still legally bound to his master who may change the degree of this economic liberty at will.

Partial liberty under slavery is well illustrated by a practice that was established in Prussia centuries ago. The masters granted their serfs two days out of the week to work for themselves. They had that degree of economic liberty.

Now suppose that the slave, instead of working directly under the guidance of his master, should be allowed to pursue elsewhere any occupation and place of employment he may choose, and to sell all his services or all the product of his toil for a money wage or a market price. With legal ownership of his slave, and with full knowledge of the slave's activities and the amount of his income, the master is able to claim all or part of the slave's earnings. If he should take three-fourths or one-half or one-fourth of it, would it then be correct to say that the underling was still three-fourths or one-half or one-fourth in economic slavery? This would seem to be essentially a correct report of the situation. The master might choose to operate this way, instead of having the slave work directly for him, if he thought that the slave would thereby produce more for the master to take away from the slave.

As another variation, suppose that several slave masters combine into a slaveholding corporation for the management of their slaves, and suppose that the corporation, rather than each of the masters separately, is delegated to direct the operation and extract the pay from the slaves. Would this lessen the degree of slavery from what it had been before? No.

As still another variation, suppose that these slaves acquire their status of slavery as a result of a popular vote among their group while they were still free men, and that the majority voted that they should all become slaves. Would this lessen the degree of slavery from their previously reported plight? No.

Suppose that the master pleads innocence of slaveholding on the grounds that he is spending the slave's earnings for what he considers to be the slave's own welfare. Would that change the degree of liberty of the slave? Is liberty to be defined in such a way as to allow me to take from you the product of your labor, so long as I claim that I shall use it for your welfare, or for the "general welfare"? Should the robbing of banks be allowable under liberty, provided the bank robbers promise to put the proceeds of the robbery to some use they claim to be worthy, or even to some use that a majority of the people have judged to be worthy?

The test of economic liberty under all these varied conditions, and others that might be listed, is to be found in the definition of economic liberty as previously explained — the right to the product of one's own labor. One who is deprived of these rights is a slave. To whatever extent he is deprived of these rights, he is to that extent a slave. And he is no less a slave because of the means of depriving him of the product of his labor.

ARE EMPLOYEES in modern society in the same position as slaves?

It is often asserted that employees are the equivalent of slaves, because the employer can pay them whatever he may desire and the employee can do nothing about it. But that is not so. There is a distinct difference between the two situations.

The slave, if he should object to his plight for any reason whatsoever, cannot move to a new situation of greater promise, nor can he leave to start a business for himself, nor can he quit work to live in retirement on his savings; he must continue to work where he is, in spite of his wishes, and continue to be subject to the dictates of the master. The employee, on the other hand, is free to make these changes; he may bargain with his employer, or he may leave for employment elsewhere, or he may start in business for himself; or he may choose to retire and not work at all, or work only part time, living on the savings he has accumulated.

But back of these differences is the one most vital to economic liberty. The employee has income of his own to spend or to save as he desires. The slave, on the other hand, does not.

An employee is not, because of that fact, a slave; nor is he the equivalent of a slave. Any employee who claims that he is the equivalent of a slave probably would not, if put to the test, willingly become a slave; the act is the test of sincerity of the belief.

The employee is, to be sure, under whatever dictates his employer chooses to impose while he is there as an employee. Presumably he has accepted this condition of employment willingly, rather than not to have that job with its pay; this is distinctly different from the plight of the slave, who was captured and held against his will and who is not free to return or to move to another job.

The employer-employee relationship amounts to this: The employer, who has the tools and other capital required for efficient production, and who presumably has the know-how of management, proposes to a prospective employee that they form a sort of partnership; the employee accepts it or not, voluntarily, dependent on whether or not he judges it to be a better prospect for him than any alternative. The employee may, in fact, take the initiative and make the original proposition to the employer because he strongly desires to cooperate in such an arrangement with one who has the tools and capital, or the know-how of management.

Whatever the route to a final deal, the employer-employee relationship is similar to two persons trading a cow and a horse, where both parties to the deal are beneficiaries. The employer, as his side of the offer, agrees to give the employee what amounts to a certain quantity of the product and a guaranteed market therefor, in exchange for the employee's services. It may turn out that the employee gets either more or less than he contributes, resulting in either a loss or a profit for the employer.

The employer-employee arrangement is in sharp contrast to that of the master-slave relationship. The slave is not offered a proposition in the original deal; he is captured.

Apparently large numbers of persons in any country prefer to be told what to do, in large areas of their lives. Large numbers cannot or do not desire, in the economic arena, to be entirely on their own; so they choose to work for others at a wage those others are willing to pay. Yet they have the essence of liberty even in this situation, for reasons that have been given.

Employees, along with those who are self-employed, have an important stake in liberty. Contemplating alternatives should make this perfectly clear.

Now WE COME to a crucial point. The question is this: If the master be the State (government, at all its levels), does the test of expropriated income still serve as a useful measure of liberty? Does the test that has been applied to a privately-owned slave still apply here?

A slave is no less a slave because of the manner by which he is deprived of the product of his own labor, and of the right to hold private property. Slavery cannot be transformed into non-slavery by having a group of owners combine to do the same thing. No matter what system is used to extract the fruits of his labors from the person, he is a free man or not (economically) to whatever extent he can or cannot have whatever he produces, to consume or to sell, to trade as he wishes for whatever he wishes, or to save as private property for later needs and uses.

This rule is still valid even when it is government that does the taking. If the government should take all that is produced, as does a master from his slave, all the citizens would then be the economic slaves of that government.

Most of the modern world has discarded the institution of private slavery, the slavery of person to person. This institution has been judged to violate the rights of persons to be free. But there is rapidly arising a form of slavery even more dangerous and deadly. The new form is more dangerous because it is more subtle, more difficult to detect and to guard against, and therefore far more widespread than personal slavery probably ever was. This is because it does not take the customary form of slavery of one person to another, as when one holds title to his slave or cattle or horses and is their unquestioned and exclusive master and owner. Therein lies the danger of this new form of slavery, a danger comparable to that of disease germs prior to the discovery of the microscope and the development of the germ theory of disease. Our present problem is to discover the equivalent of the microscope for use in diagnosing the causes of the economic diseases of our society whereby liberty is lost, and to develop the means of identification of the germs which cause those diseases.

The superstition prevails that if the government takes from unwilling people the product of their labor to pay for governmental costs of which they disapprove, it becomes a commendable act unlike that of the master taking from his slave. Especially is the taking supposed to be proper if it occurs in a "democratic" nation. It is as though we should rule, by custom or by law, that robbery becomes a commendable act if a large enough number of people approve of it and engage in it.

The mere fact of taxes having been paid is no test of basic willingness; it is no evidence that a form of slavery does not exist, as a result of the displacement of voluntary action in the free market of choice. The fact that a slave works in his master's field, similarly, is no evidence that slavery is not involved. The giving of one's wallet to the hold-up robber without a struggle of conspicuous conflict is no evidence that the robbery did not take place. In all these instances there is an overhanging threat which causes the seemingly peaceful submission; the unfortunate victim is allowed no alternative consistent with liberty. In the case of taxes, the act of non-payment results in a legal claim against one's property and future income, presumably far greater in amount than the tax bill under protest.

"The power to tax is the power to destroy."

The Chinese scholar, Chang Hsin-hai, in his article on "The Moral Basis of World Peace," asserts that this disease of our society stems from a double standard of morals. He says that the root of our troubles, both national and international, lies in the acceptance of moral standards in government totally different from those accepted and demonstrated as necessary for a good society so far as individual conduct is concerned. If a politician, either national or international, engages in practices and policies which in individual conduct would be considered as most contemptible, he is commonly honored for his "progressiveness and farsightedness, and for the great service he is rendering to the citizens of his country." He is elected again and again to public office, even though the same practices by the operator of a private grocery store or a farm would lead to his being all but run out of town.

At the root of the double standard of moral conduct, to which Chang Hsin-hai refers, is the accepted belief that many forms of predatory practice, when conducted under the name of government, are honorable acts. On that premise has been built a progressive encroachment on the liberty of individuals, which passes as "progressive" in politics. Governments in recent times have taken more and more of the product of persons' labor "for the common good." But by the mere fact of its taking, the government is thereby engaging more and more in the enslavement of the citizens. If this process had involved the complete enslavement of certain persons, it would be more noticeable and we would then be able to see it in its true light.

As ONE ASPECT of the problem of lost liberty and double standards of conduct, the government is getting more and more into business in a manner condemned in private practice. This fact must be observed in any discussion of the status of liberty in our time, even at the risk of not being fully understood in a cursory treatment of an involved question.

Nearly every business operated by government has these features:

1. They are monopolies.

2. Their initial capital is obtained through the force and power of taxation.

3. They need not operate efficiently, nor be able to cover their costs in order to stay in business, because they can always fall back on their taxing power to make up the difference between their performance and the people's direct appraisal of its worth.

All three violate liberty in one way or another.

How would you like to compete in private business with someone who could force you to put up his initial capital and who could send you a bill for all his losses?

As an individual citizen, it is no defense against the loss of liberty to say that you are a citizen and have a share of ownership in these governmental projects. You will find, for instance, that you are a shareholder in the Spruce Production Corporation, one of the federal government's hundreds of corporations which now have a total of over $30 billion of capital assets. Try some day to sell your "ownership" share in that project.

As another illustration, United States citizens — including tee-totalers — are forced to support a budgeted deficit to pay for the federal production of rum in the Virgin Islands. One who does not care for this investment is forced to invest in it anyhow. He is not even allowed to shift his investment to some other governmental project that is more appealing to him; and if he were allowed to shift, it would make no difference anyhow because the set-up precludes enjoying any of the privileges of ownership in its real sense.

What, in any practical sense, do you have to say about who is to be the manager of "your" corporation? What sense is there to calling it ownership if you cannot sell it, and if in addition you can be assessed for its financial failures indefinitely into the future?

The corollary of the right of ownership is the right of dis-ownership. So if I cannot sell a thing, it is evident that I do not really own it. Can a Russian citizen, who becomes dissatisfied with his part of the Russian system of socialistic "ownership in common," sell his share of Russia some day and convert the proceeds into some other form of real wealth?

This matter of government in business must come under thorough review by anyone who would consider the status of liberty in our time. Strange as it may sound, it comprises an increasingly important aspect of the modern version of slavery. Any measure of lost liberty must include it, because it is one of the forms of delusion under which, as Burke said, people give up their liberties.

CHAPTER THIRTEEN

THE EXTENT OF LOST LIBERTY

A ROUGH MEASUREMENT of the encroachment on liberty is to be found, then, in the proportion of the product of a person's labor that is taken from him by force or by threat of force, by government. A study of these figures, over the century and a half of our history as a nation, gives cause for deep concern (see chart on page 108).[1]

In 1947 the figure for governmental take was 29 cents from each dollar of income, or one and one-half times the entire food bill of the nation (excluding the taxes buried in the price of food).[2] A common reaction may be, "Perhaps so, but I don't pay any such amount in taxes." Much of this tax is in the form of hidden taxes, and one cannot see what is hidden. About two-thirds of this 29 cents, or about $1,000 in a year for the average family, is in the form of various hidden taxes; this amount of tax has become buried in the prices of everything you buy and of every serv-

[1] For detailed comments on the history of these changes, see 31¢, by F. A. Harper, (Irvington, New York: The Foundation for Economic Education, 1947).

[2] The figure includes "loans" by the United States Government to foreign nations, because past experiences and present conditions in these foreign governments suggest that repayment is highly questionable.

LOSS OF FREE CHOICE IN THE SPENDING OF INCOMES
Figures prior to 1849 include Federal Government only

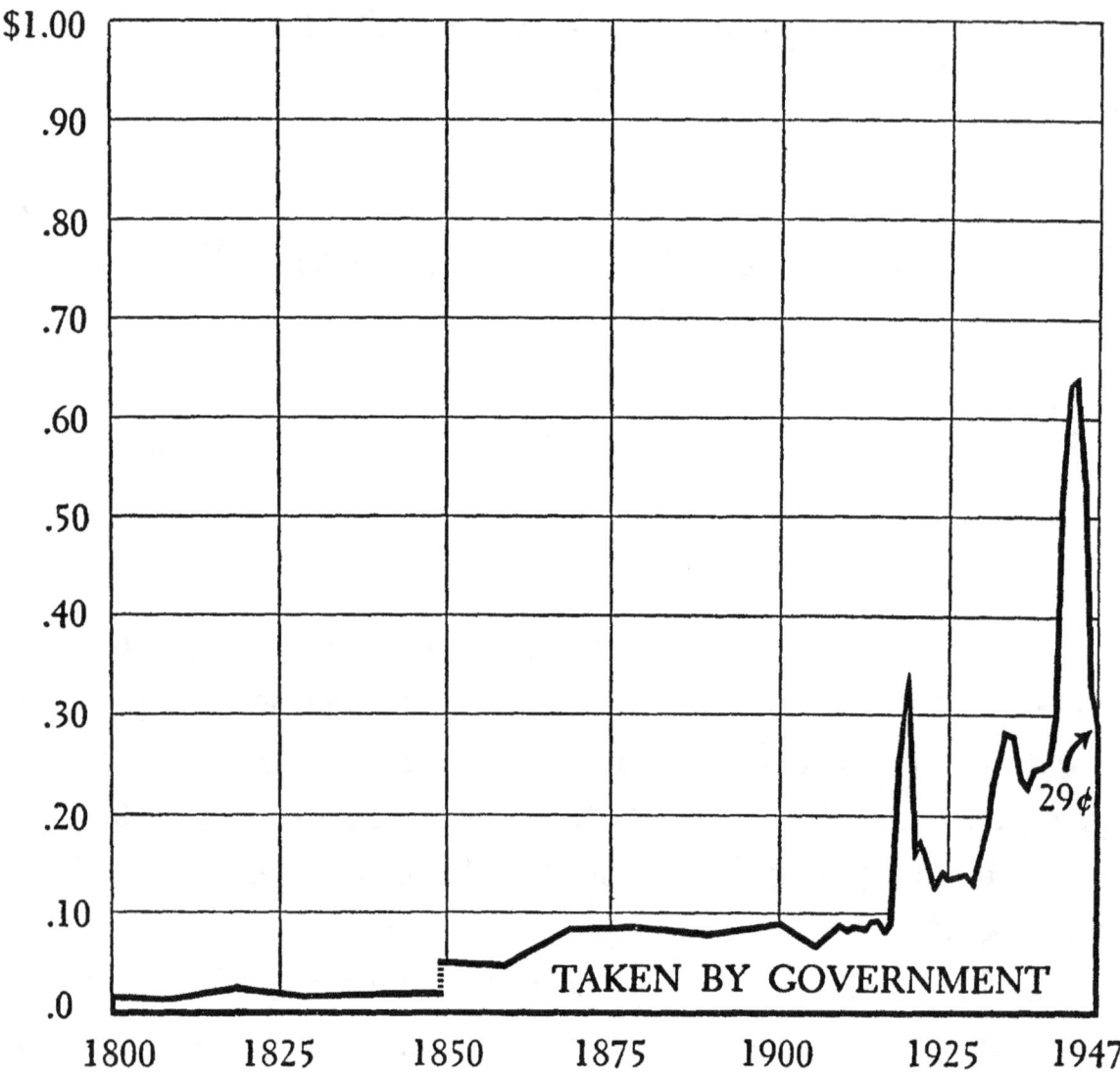

ice you employ — bread, shoes, haircuts, electric bill, the new car, movies, railroad tickets — everything. One author has estimated that there are 502 taxes on a pair of shoes. When all of these hidden taxes are brought to light, one finds that he now works 3½ months for the government, leaving only 8½ months to work for himself.

Government in the United States is now taking from persons' incomes an amount equivalent to the complete enslavement of about 42 million persons — working persons and members of their families. Compare that figure, and the concern about it, with the figure of 4 million privately-owned slaves in the United States at the outbreak of the War Between the States!

All this is being done under the name of liberty, in a nation where liberty supposedly reigns as a beacon for the rest of an enslaved world. It is all being done under the name of a "progressive" society.

The present figure of 29 cents, even under present conditions of high employment and money incomes, is frightening enough. But a decline in employment to a point like that of 1938-40, in its effect on the national income, would automatically increase the burden to 35 cents or more out of each dollar of persons' incomes; and this estimate fails to include any additional governmental costs "to relieve the depression."

The threat and danger embodied in a figure of 35 cents, or more, can be gleaned from a few comparisons. The latest figure at hand for the United Kingdom is about 35 cents out of each dollar.[3] The situation in the United Kingdom under this burden is well known, as suggested by the common use of the word "austerity," and also by the fact that the United States is being asked to contribute great sums of money in the hope of bolstering the British economy.

A study of the tax burden of 48 nations in the late twenties offers some sobering evidence.[4] Among those 48 nations were four large ones (over 25 million population) where the government was then taking more than 20 per cent of the citizen's income. Call to mind what has happened in those four countries from the standpoint of liberty of the citizens:

---

[3] Derived from figures in "National Income and Expenditure of the United Kingdom," His Majesty's Stationery Office, London, 1947, and other sources.

The London Economist for March 19, 1949 reported that the figure for the current budget has risen further to 40 per cent of the total of all incomes.

[4] Edmond E. Lincoln, "Sobering Realities Regarding Tax Burdens," The Commercial and Financial Chronicle (April 1, 1948).

	Taxes as per cent of national income, 1929-1930
USSR	29
Germany	22
France	21
United Kingdom	21

A near-comparable figure for the United States at that time was 14 per cent, as the cost of government in proportion to the national income.

"The power to tax is the power to destroy." The power to tax incomes is the power to destroy incomes. The power to tax property is the power to destroy property, whether by a capital levy or in any other form. And since income and property are the economic extensions of the person, the power to tax becomes the power to destroy persons to whatever extent economic considerations are important to life and happiness.

In an autocracy, the power to tax is the power of the autocrat to destroy persons in this sense. In a democracy, the power to tax becomes the power of certain persons to destroy other persons, and it becomes the right to use all forms of legalized power and influence to do so — lobbies, pressure groups, and all the others.

Dr. Colin Clark, the Australian economist, has concluded from his study of governmental costs that whenever the figure for any country rises to more than 20 or 25 per cent, progressive inflation and the debauchery of the currency is the likely result.[5]

And Lord Keynes reported:

Lenin is said to have declared that the best way to destroy the Capitalist System was to debauch the currency. By a continuing process of inflation, governments can confiscate, secretly and unobserved, an important part of the wealth of their citizens.[6]

[5] Dr. Colin Clark, "Public Finance and Changes in the Value of Money," *The Economic Journal* (December, 1945).

[6] John Maynard Keynes, *The Economic Consequences of the Peace* (New York: Harcourt, Brace and Howe, 1920, p. 235).

The "Capitalist System," which Lenin wished to destroy, is based on the right to the product of one's own labor and on the right to save some of it as private property. It is based on the foundation of liberty, as herein defined.

The private property that comes into being when a person spends less than his income, or consumes for purposes of his current living less than he produces, becomes the capital of the "Capitalist System." This right to private security in the form of one's savings put to some productive use, is the essence of economic liberty. Destroying the "Capitalist System" means destroying this liberty and these rights; it means the prohibition of the self-responsibility and private security, in the form of personal savings; it means a most powerful invitation to personal irresponsibility and intemperance in economic consumption.

History confirms the effectiveness of these means of destroying the foundations of human liberty. And it further records the failures of socialistic nations of the past, in sharp contrast with the human happiness and progress that abounds wherever a high degree of human liberty prevails.

Events before the French Revolution illustrate the consequences of economic intemperance. Following a long series of governmental deficits, the debt by 1788 had reached such proportions that, with an added deficit of 20 per cent of governmental expenditures in that year, half of the budget went for costs of the debt.[7] The cost of the debt would have exceeded even that proportion, except for the "shameless waste" and extravagance that padded the remaining portion of expenditures. Taxes, though having been raised to the limit of yield, were far from enough to pay the costs of this wastage and the pensioning of privilege and favoritism. Indirect taxes, including inflating the currency to pay

[7] Georges Lefebvre, The Coming of the French Revolution (Princeton University Press, 1947, p. 22).

expenses, was used more and more. The credit standing of the government finally was completely destroyed, so that income from the issuance of loans was no longer possible. The government extended its monopolies and confiscated wealth in various ways. Personal violence began and spread as a consequence of enforcing the decrees and as an accompaniment of the growing economic vice, until the bloody revolution was in full swing.

Among the authorities on the subject of liberty in relation to the rise and fall of civilizations is Sir Flinders Petrie, the great British archeologist. He traced the six great civilizations of the world during the last 8,000 years. He found that the rise of these civilizations occurred while liberty was at its height, that when economic parasitism set in these civilizations degenerated rapidly into a long period of "dark ages."

That, in a nutshell, indicates the present status of liberty in the United States.

Many persons who call themselves realists, but who are called fatalists by others, know these events of history and believe that liberty in a nation tends to erode more and more until finally it has been almost entirely lost. Whereas it seems that such has tended to be the pattern of national experience, no one pattern is inevitable as the course of a national society. If it were inevitable, why would there be all the variation of patterns between nations now and at any other time in the past? This argument of inevitability becomes an effective weapon of those who are pleased with recent trends in this and in other countries, and who would like to have all opposition to their hopes fade before the "inevitable."

The lovers of liberty must remember that, in a seriously ill society as with a seriously ill person, the choice may be between some form of early medical treatment — perhaps pills that may be unpalatable at the moment — and the services of an undertaker. If these preventive steps are not taken in time, and if the little problems of liberty are allowed to go unsolved, they accumulate into catastrophe; in the end there comes bloody revolution of the worst sort, when the growing octopus of tyranny has finally become unbearable.

The great social problem of our age is that of designing the preventive medicine that will stop the eroding liberty in the body politic. Further, once the disease has advanced to the point of a most serious danger, a bitter curative medicine is required to regain already-lost liberty.

PART 3

THE PRESENT PROBLEM

If the true spark of religious and civil liberty be kindled, it will burn. Human agency cannot extinguish it. Like the earth's central fire, it may be smothered for a time; the ocean may overwhelm it; mountains may press it down; but its inherent and unconquerable force will heave both the ocean and the land, and at some time or other, in some place or other, the volcano will break out and flame up to heaven.

DANIEL WEBSTER

CHAPTER FOURTEEN

SPECIAL PRIVILEGE

With government in the United States taking 29 cents of each dollar of a person's income at the present time—an amount identical with that for the USSR in 1929-1930 — what is to be done?

In considering any new proposals for governmental expenditures, and in reviewing those that now exist, this should be the guiding rule: Grants of special privilege to any person or group of persons should be denied, because these grants can be made only by infringement on the rights of others — on liberty. "Benefits" for this and "benefits" for that should be denied. The granting of any of the so-called benefits by government violates the foundation of liberty — that a person should have the right to the product of his own labor, and the right to dispose of it or to keep any part of it as he desires.

No attempt will be made here to list the numerous forms of special privilege now in operation. Each person can do that for himself, and if there should be a difference of opinion over an item, the difference could not be resolved by a mere listing of the item in question.

The nature of special privilege, however, should be clear in its main outlines. Special privilege is any item of income or of position in the market for goods and services where the amount paid and received fails to reflect the judgment of "the judges of the market place" as to its worth. It is where the judgment of the voters in the economic market place is overruled by their political servants; it is where persons are forced to pay for a thing beyond their opinion of its worth, through the device of an authority backed by the taxing power or legal penalty.

Among the things that fall in this class of special privilege are monopoly, prohibition of competition through force, fixing of prices by governmental decree or protection of others who do the same thing, the forcing of payment for work not wanted done, and the prohibition of the free movement of goods across political borders.

The government, having no independent source of income except what it takes from the incomes of the citizens, cannot give a "benefit" to any one person either as a direct transfer of money or in any other way without correspondingly denying another the right to the product of his labor. Some evening when there is nothing else to do, an interesting occupation would be to take a copy of the federal budget and study the projects reported therein as they fail to meet this test of special privilege. It would provide plenty of food for thought.

On a recent occasion when discussing a proposal involving a major program of special privilege, a well known person said that the only thing he could see against it was the cost. Its entire cost would unavoidably have to be paid in full by the taxpayer. It is common to speak as though this cost aspect can be dismissed lightly as a minor detail. One might as illogically say that his wife wants seven mink coats; that the idea seems to him to be a good one — except for the detail of its cost. Why is the matter of cost any less relevant when the item is under the scope of government?

"The power to tax is the power to destroy." Special privilege is of necessity the process of destruction in operation, always and everywhere.

THE MATTER OF STRATEGY by persons, both individually and through their organizations, becomes highly important if there is a sincere desire to assist in the recovery of liberty.

An attitude which over the decades has contributed more and more to the loss of liberty is one that may be called "compensatory parasitism." That high-sounding phrase refers, in more simple terms, to the philosophy of: You parasitize me and I'll parasitize you." It is the philosophy that one evil justifies another.

The effects of this policy abound on every hand. The government becomes a grab-bag and one citizen justifies his becoming a parasite by observing that others are doing it. "So-and-so is getting a hand-out from the government; why shouldn't I?"

A cardinal principle of successful parasitism is that the number of parasites must be kept low. Otherwise the host is killed and the parasites must die.

The wolf pack operates as a form of parasitic economy. They live constantly in a meager existence, and some of them must die as their number increases relative to the sheep they plunder and kill.

Our economy is not like that of a pack of wolves, which plunders but does not produce. Ours is a productive rather than a parasitic economy. The basis of a free society is the absence of parasitism.

So the point of strategy is this: Why not encourage a complete about-face in policy among all thinking citizens and all leaders of thought? Why not oppose special privilege for each and every person and group, rather than try to acquire compensatory parasitism for one's self?

If the principle of "no special privilege" is to prevail, it will be necessary to support that principle in its every application as a principle. It should be adopted as a uniform rule, across the board.

CHAPTER FIFTEEN

RECOVERING LIBERTY

THE FASHION OF THE TIMES seems to be to "resign to the inevitable." Some say that the wise thing to do is to relax and try to grab as much as possible for one's self, while the nation declines into the abyss of collectivism. Anyone devoted to the principles of liberty will refuse to accept that solution; he will refuse to accept it on both moral and practical grounds. The plight of peoples all over the world where compromise and "resignation to the inevitable" has been the adopted solution should be ample evidence of what is in store if we continue to pursue that course. The prospect is not a pretty picture. No liberal will want any part in this route to the destruction of liberty.

Let us take a practical look at "resigning ourselves to the inevitable," in economic terms. If we should adopt a policy of social parasitism, and if it were possible to divide up the entire supposed wealth of this nation and consume it as a pack of wolves would devour a sheep, there would be only enough on a valuation basis in these "fabulously wealthy" United States to sustain our present level of living for 3½ years. The estimated wealth of the nation, in other words, is only 3½ times the estimated worth of the goods and services produced in a year. So, if all these items of wealth were actually "consumables," like those we eat and use in current consumption, there is only enough to sustain our present level of living for 3½ years. Thereafter, the wealth which is now responsible for at least nine-tenths of our output of goods and services would all be gone; those who survived the resulting privation would then have to exist on what they could produce under the economic sterility that would then prevail, by using primitive methods that would probably yield less than one-tenth of the level of living we now enjoy. When viewed in this light, "resigning to the inevitable" is seen to be a disastrous form of surrender.

"But we shall divide up only a part of the wealth, not all of it." The evil effect will still be there, though in a lesser degree. Economic parasitism does not become a good thing when lessened in degree; it becomes only a less serious evil.

Our present society rests on a foundation totally different from that of a pack of wolves, and any undermining of its foundations will result in its collapse. Furthermore, the higher any society has risen, like ours, the greater the debacle whenever the loss of liberty undermines it.

This discussion has been mainly of the economic and material aspects of the problem; but it is not meant to imply that these economic aspects are the only aspects or even the most important ones. If Hume's views are right — and I have no evidence that they are wrong — it is important to be ever mindful that the foundations of liberty embrace the foundations of justice and morals, and of a moral civilization. The most highly prized aspects of liberty are these, and the economic welfare that develops under liberty is but a pleasant, extra dividend flowing therefrom.

IF LOST LIBERTY is to be regained, the general course to be followed is simple. Liberties that have been taken away from individuals must be restored; there can be no other answer. Whether it be started with this or that liberty is a detail, however important. The way to start is to start somewhere.

The solution of the problem of liberty requires that a sizable number of thought-leaders grasp a wholly new attitude on matters of government. There must be a change from the belief that has increasingly prevailed during twenty years or more in this nation, and for a longer time in other countries like Germany and Britain which now stand as pathetic demonstrations of the effects of lost liberty. It is not enough to blame our congressmen and to expect them to do the job of regaining lost liberty alone. Weeds the size of sequoia trees have grown up in our vineyard of liberty, and one cannot eliminate a forest of sequoia trees by using a jack-knife at the tips of the branches.

The present year's budget for the federal government weighs about half more than the Sears, Roebuck or Montgomery Ward catalogues; it contains 1534 pages; on each page, on the average, is information about $26 million of expenditures. Suppose that a congressman is charged with the task of reviewing that budget and cutting out all "non-essentials," and suppose that he were to take one hour to study each million dollars of expenditure — truly a cursory study of an expenditure of that amount of money. A congressman, spending full time at it, would be able to finish the job in about 21 years, or about 1970! He would then be ready to start a similar review of the budgets of the remaining 30,000 units of government, other than the federal, in the United States. That indicates the impossible task which confronts the law makers; it is not surprising that they bog down under it.

What conclusion can one draw other than that the hope of citizens' supervision of governmental expenditures of $57 billion a year by the "democratic process" is a futile hope, no matter how it is attempted? It is foolish to expect to recover liberty in that manner. When once the power of free choice in the spending of their incomes has been abandoned by the citizens, and these economic rights surrendered to government, their liberty will have gone with it; it makes no difference how the governmental procedure is designed. Either you spend your own income as you deem best or someone spends it for you in some way that he deems best, and there is no alternative. The hope that 145 million persons can maintain control over such a stupendous expenditure, merely by the device of a few of them going to the polls once in a while, is pure fantasy. Until it is realized to be a fantasy, we are destined to pursue futility, buoyed only by a little fleeting hope every two or four years at election time.

What, then, is to be done? After liberty has been lost beyond a certain point, its recovery is difficult by peaceful means. The peaceful solution is to unwind the accumulated powers of government over the lives and incomes of the citizens.

Eternal vigilance is not now enough; it is too late for that to be adequate, for the same reason that eternal vigilance of the barn door is no help after the horse has been stolen. Nor is the changing of top personnel in the government, or "reform governments," any answer to the basic problem. The gaining of better administration of an evil in the form of unwarranted power is a victory without virtue. The most efficient and best possible administration of slavery will not transform it into liberty.

A blueprint for the procedure of unwinding an illiberal government, even if I knew exactly the order in which it should proceed, is impossible here. But the principle that should guide the process is: No special privilege, no trading of special privileges.

"BUT WHAT can I do? Yours is a negative program of do-nothingness. I want to support a positive program!"

Suppose that the question at issue was that of a proposed murder, by shooting. Your objection to it is met with the rebuff:

"All right, how do you propose that he be murdered?" Believing as you do that murder by any means is wrong, it would seem foolish to offer as a "positive" suggestion that the murder be by drowning. The objection is to murder by any means and by any "administration." The positive program is that it not be done at all; that abstaining from the act is the wise course of action.

If such a stand is to be accused of being obstructionist tactics, and of putting obstacles in the path of progress, one must then conclude that the accuser differs on the very fundamentals of the matter. He must believe murder to be a good and justifiable act, which then reduces the question in his mind to that of a choice between various means of committing the murder and other administrative details of carrying it out.

Dealing with the issues of the day from the standpoint of liberty is similar. When the advocate of liberty speaks with disfavor about some program that would violate liberty, he is likely to be met with this sincere and well-intentioned rebuff: "Your objection seems to be well reasoned, and I'm inclined to accept it, but how do you propose that the program be set up?" The answer is that, consistent with liberty, you would have no "program" in the sense of which he thus speaks of "positive action."

To one who believes in liberty, liberty is a positive program of the highest order. To one who believes otherwise, the only "positive" program is that which is destructive of liberty.

If, however, one with a basic faith in liberty fails to know its processes-in-action so well that he can solve the daily issues consistent with liberalism, he will constantly be pulled offside in the game of its defense. He will keep falling into the trap of being led to select one or another method of violating liberty, and he will thereby assist others in its destruction. If that destruction be the result of ignorance rather than of an unintentional mistake, the result will be the same and liberty will be destroyed.

So the first thing to be done by all of us with a basic faith in liberty is to acquire an understanding of it so thorough that adoption in daily practice becomes clear and automatic, like the things we do in our daily occupational duties. This degree of understanding is not easy. It is not to be bought in the store with nickels and dimes. Its understanding must be acquired in the same manner as that of any other complex subject, through long and careful study and thought.

To one who has acquired a mastery of the subject of liberty to that extent, action consistent with liberty will become a positive program, supported by considered reasons. He will know why the so-called "positive" programs, currently so popular, are programs that destroy liberty. Then, without self-consciousness and with a feeling of pride rather than of shame, he will take a clear and firm position against each and every means of destroying or diluting liberty, oblivious to appealing but false claims in which they may be clothed.

One will have then become capable of helping his friends toward a better understanding of liberty, without resorting to the futile process of voicing mere conclusions or platitudes that are lacking in the force of real understanding. Only in that way will knowledge spread to those who seek help and guidance, to those who are in search of honest answers to perplexing problems.

This method is, to be sure, slow. But there are no shortcuts to liberty. Shortcuts taken in a haste for action usually violate the basic tenets of liberty in the process, and for that reason they lead one further from his intended goal.

Correct action automatically follows understanding — the only route to correct action. Nothing else will serve. If this process seems hopelessly slow, there should be the sustaining faith that liberty is in harmony with truth, and with the intended design of the human social order. Truth is immortal, despite the defeats that it seems to suffer along the way. Truth has a power that is no respecter of persons, nor of the numbers of persons who may at any time be in darkness about truth. Truth has a power that cannot be touched by physical force. It is impossible to shoot a truth.

THE LOVER OF LIBERTY will find ways to be free.

APPENDICES

The spirit of liberty is the spirit which is not too sure that it is right. The spirit of liberty is the spirit which seeks to understand the minds of other men and women. The spirit of liberty is the spirit which weighs their interests alongside its own without bias. The spirit of liberty remembers that not even a sparrow falls to earth unheeded. The spirit of liberty is the spirit of Him who, near 2,000 years ago, taught mankind that lesson it has never learned, but has never quite forgotten; that there may be a kingdom where the least shall be heard and considered side by side with the greatest.

JUDGE LEARNED HAND

FAITHS ABOUT THE NATURE AND DESTINY OF MAN

> Before people can be persuaded to abandon one faith they must be given something else to grab hold of as a means of salvation. Men cannot live without faith in something.
>
> JOHN RUSTGARD

THIS DISCUSSION of liberty is predicated on certain faiths regarding mankind.

However much it may be regretted that an analysis must be started on the "uncertain footing" of faiths, this is unavoidable. What we "know" is ever bounded on all sides by what we do not know. In the dimension of space, for instance, what can be viewed is bounded by what is unviewed; that which lies beyond must be dealt with in terms of theory or faith, as to its content and form. It is the same with all aspects other than space.

Despite man's efforts to master ignorance and press back the boundaries of the unknown, there shall remain an unconquered and unknown portion until such a time as we may have gained an insight into everything between the primal mist and the end of eternity. Until then, faith will have to continue to bridge the unknown. The concepts which one holds have to be constructed within these faiths, and any analysis must rest on some working hypotheses.

Faiths are not debatable in terms of scientific reasoning. One faith, in that sense, stands equal to any other so far as "proof" is concerned. A faith may be based on "hunch," or on "instinct," or on the authority of someone admired and trusted in these respects. But whatever its origin, it is held with deep conviction until replaced by something accepted as more tenable. It is for these reasons that faiths serve well to illustrate the impropriety and unwisdom of authoritarianism.

The following are the faiths, or hypotheses on which this analysis of liberty is based. They relate to the nature and destiny of man.

1. There exists a Supernatural, which guides the affairs of the universe.

2. In the design of the universe, everything is subject to certain natural laws which rule without being subject to revocation by any human or any combination of humans; among them are "physical law" as well as "moral law"; these laws, and the events that occur under their ruling guidance, constitute what we call truth.

3. Humans intuitively act in harmony with these natural laws, both physically and morally; failure to do so is the result of ignorance rather than of inclination; thus it is concluded that man is basically "good," and will do the right thing provided he is given the correct "facts" and is left free to follow his instincts without interference; if it were not so, it would be difficult to explain man's survival and his capacity for progress.

4. Law, and other social guides to conduct, must be in harmony with natural law, if serious consequences are to be avoided; obedience to any other guides for conduct — guides that are in disharmony with natural law — must carry the penalty meted out by the court of Higher Justice which can be neither bought nor influenced by untruths.

5. Each person is a self-responsible, independent unit who is obligated to answer only to the Supernatural Authority, in any final sense; he must answer to the natural laws of the universe; no person or persons may rightfully intercede between him and his God, with any rights of unchecked power over the other person; there is no place for any "Divine Right of Kings," by that or by any other name, in this order of things; whomever attempts to claim that right is attempting to forge the Supernatural and is therefore engaged in trespassing on the rights of another person or persons.

6. The individual has no bounden duty to serve some intangible "common good" or "society," in violation of what seems to him to be the best thing to do; one's obligation is to his conscience, and to the Supernatural Order as he interprets it, rather than to abdicate this responsibility and attempt to shift it to others in political office or to some abstraction in the form of some organization; no person, under guise of these conjured abstractions, has the right to obligate another person to something or to someone unknown specifically to him; and any person who attempts to do so is an impostor attempting somehow to gain power for himself in exchange for the promise that he can free another from unavoidable self-responsibilities.

7. A person's capacity to perceive the nature of these natural laws, which rule his being, is limited by his intelligence or powers of instinctive conduct; his beliefs, in this respect, are both his privilege and his responsibility; he is free to choose his sources of information as guides in his search for truth, and he is personally responsible for the wisdom of that choice and for the resulting conclusions; he will know that no person, not even himself, has any direct and certain line of communication with the sources of truth; all conclusions carry a corresponding uncertainty no matter who holds them; he knows that while he cannot avoid acting

on the basis of some belief, these beliefs must ever be held subject to change as further evidence or new reasoning becomes available; but always he is obligated, by honesty, to believe and act in accordance with truth as he then sees it.

It is within this structure of faiths, as working hypotheses, that liberty is herein discussed.

PATTERNS OF VARIATION

VARIATION SEEMS to pervade the universe. Even where once it was believed not to exist, further study and refinement of measurement reveals its presence.

When one views the members of another race, with which he is unfamiliar, they all seem to be alike until on further acquaintance their differences come to be more and more evident to him; eventually he finds them to be as great as the differences among members of his own race. It is the same with other species of life, and with the unlive formations of nature.

Once it was believed that the physical unit, the atom, lacked variation but now physicists are said to believe that even atoms vary. Everywhere variation seems to exist, in everything.

The complexity of compounded variation surpasses our comprehension. A person's fingerprint will distinguish him from every other person; or a toe print; or the hairs on his head; and so on through a long list of features, each of which exhibits differences. When these features are considered in their seemingly endless number of combinations, the differences between any two persons is found to be so great that one wonders how any similarity between any two persons is to be noticed. It should be clear that a knowledge of variation causes the "average man" to dissolve into an abstraction, not found modeled anywhere in actual life.

Variation, in its rough and crude expression of random occurences, seems to be disorderly and chaotic. When observed in this form, it seems to be the result of pure "chance," and to deny any purpose; it seems to reveal nothing but the "carelessness of nature." But we shall see that this interpretation is highly doubtful.

A little over a century ago the foundations were laid for a science of the phenomenon of variation by the French mathematician Laplace (1749-1827). He began the work of dealing with variations so as to reveal the similarities of their patterns.

The newly developing science of variation was applied to astronomy by Carl Friedrich Gauss (1777-1855), the German mathematician and astronomer.

Adolphe Quetelet (1796-1855), the Belgian, deserves credit for the general principles of variation, reported in works published in 1835 and later. Though an astronomer, he extended his studies of variation to many other types of data such as temperature, the price of grain, and the heights and chest-measurements of men. Quetelet's findings led to what later became known as the "normal curve" of variation.

The normal curve exhibits a symmetrical mathematical series. When graphed, it becomes a smoothly bell-shaped curve. About two-thirds of the total area of this curve lies within vertical lines placed at a distance of one standard deviation on each side of the vertical center, or the average of the series of data.

Quetelet found that all the data he studied fitted this style of curve fairly well.

The super-salesman of this new concept of order within the seeming chaos of variation, and of the predictable nature of variation, was Francis Galton. In 1899, in his classic book on *Natural Inheritance*, he had this to say:

It is difficult to understand why statisticians commonly limit their inquiries to Averages, and do not revel in more comprehensive views. Their souls seem as dull to the charm of variety as that of the native of one of our flat English counties, whose retrospect of Switzerland was that, if its mountains could be thrown into its lakes, two nuisances would be got rid of at once. An Average is but a solitary fact, whereas if a single other fact be added to it, an entire Normal Scheme, which nearly corresponds to the observed one, starts potentially into existence.

And:

It [the "normal curve" of variation] reigns with serenity and in complete self-effacement amidst the wildest confusion. . . . Whenever a large sample of chaotic elements are taken in hand and marshalled in the order of their magnitudes, an unsuspected and most beautiful form of regularity proves to have been latent all along.

Galton asserted that this knowledge of the nature of variation, had it been known in ancient Greece, would most certainly have been personified and deified. And so it might. Galton himself spoke of it as being of a cosmic order.

Galton, as one of the pioneers in the discovery and interpretation of variation, may be excused for what now appears to be over-simplification. It now appears that the "normal curve" type of pattern in variation is not the only one. More accurately, as we now believe, Galton might well have waxed eloquent about the laws of variation in possible designs where more than a single pattern is allowed to unfold itself. These variations, in more than the single pattern of which Galton spoke, all have within them an orderliness which is concealed by their usually shuffled arrangement. Variation in each instance seems to fit into one or another mathematical function of the variable.

One formation of variables, more pertinent than the "normal curve" to many of the matters with which the social scientists deal, is that found in income variations and wealth variations. It is the "harmonic series" of magnitudes, wherein, if we represent the largest as 1, the second largest will be found to be ½, the third largest ⅓, the fourth largest ¼. . . .

The presence of this curve is revealed in its pattern from the largest end of the array, where large size and low frequency is found, to the other end where small size and high frequency is found. A tolerance must be allowed for the latter end of the array, in essentially all instances of data that has been derived from observed events. This is because wherever the law of limitation applies — which is universal except in things like distance or time, where observations are of unlimited magnitude — the harmonic series runs out and the frequency falls off unavoidably; the result is, under these conditions, the appearance of a "skewed curve."

The pattern of variability of the harmonic type appears over a wide range of phenomenon. Vilfredo Pareto (1848-1923) found it to prevail among income data. In addition to income and wealth, it appears in the demand for any product or service, in the size of cities and towns in any settled national unit, in the frequency in the use of various words by one person, to mention a few that have been studied. We may even suspect to find that the harmonic series describes the variation of human abilities, as will be revealed only when an over-all measurement of ability has been developed.

One further point should be mentioned about variation. The fact that variation seems to fit into certain definite patterns as to type (the "normal curve," the harmonic series, etc.) does not mean that the intensity of variation is the same wherever the pattern is the same. On the contrary, the intensity of variation differs widely. The size of one species of animal varies more intensely than another; the weight of one species of life varies more intensely than another; the color of one species of flower varies more intensely than another. . . . It is found, for instance, that the seedlings of the apple are highly variable in their commonly-observed characteristics, whereas the seeds of some other plants yield much more similar offspring.

VARIATION AND CHANGE

THE PATTERNS found to exist in variation suggest that their presence has a purpose.

Without changes in the weather and other things, physical and chemical changes could not occur in the world. Except for variation among the chromosomes, offspring would all be identical with their parents and the form of life would remain unchanged over the ages.

The principle of change may be stated this way: There is no way to win a race without differences; there would, in fact, be no purpose in having a race in the first place except for the presence of differences to be tested.

Variation gives rise to change, in two ways:
1. Selection and discard
2. Combining

The process of selection can be illustrated by the stone-age man's selection of a stone best suited, by size and other qualities, to the making of a weapon; or by the selection of stone for a building; or by the selection of a candidate for a job. An unselected item falls into discard, for that particular purpose. The wisdom of the selection affects the outcome. Without variation, change by selection and discard would be impossible.

The other method by which variation results in change is combination. Reproduction among living things, both sexual and asexual, is of this type. Combining non-living things by mixture or by compounding, as with chemicals, is another type. In any of these forms, variation in the "parentage" gives rise to change in the "offspring." Without variation these changes could not occur.

Changes might further be classified as to whether or not choice, or the exercise of preference, guided by either instinct or intelligence, is involved. Variation in the weather, for instance, lacking anything like human choice as its cause, has given rise to events of transcendent importance like the glaciers and the seasons, erosion and typhoons. But the selection of a mate is quite a different matter, so far as the exercise of choice is concerned. Some of the biological processes seem to be in the pale between these two types, because we know so little about them.

Changes may be rapid or slow, dependent on many things. The more ruthless the process of discard under selection, the more rapid the change — either for better or worse.[1] And likewise, the more divergent the items that are mixed or crossed by combination, the more rapid will be the expected change.

The "higher" the form of life or of non-life composition, the more complex its variation and the more rapid the expected change that follows from crossing two of them. As the complexity increases, the "offspring" become less and less predictable. In chemistry, for instance, combinations of the ninety-odd different basic elements can result in innumerable compounds; possible mixtures of different possible compounds, in turn, magnifies beyond our capacity for comprehension the number of possible results. It is similar for the complex living organisms, like persons, where differences combine in the biological process into innumer-

---

[1] Matter is not, of course, destructible; it only changes form. But it is the question of form about which we are speaking here — a certain species of form.

able and wide differences. That is why persons differ so widely in their capacity to do different things, to comprehend different things, or to contribute to progress.

Out of this change comes "progress." And the greater the variation, the more rapid the progress can be. It makes no difference, so far as the opportunity for progress is concerned, whether the change is induced by the Unseen Hand of evolution, or by conscious choice as in the selection of a mate, or by learning from someone who is more informed, or by simply patterning one's acts after those who know better how to do a thing.

The process of selection from among variation, by design and intelligent choice of persons, is an old and well-known source of progress. It is in this manner that better varieties of plants and animals have been selected to replace those less adapted, less resistant to disease and less efficient.

More recently variation has been induced by "cross breeding" and "induced mutation," in order that more rarely outstanding new strains may be discovered and propagated. Most mutations are short-lived, self-destructive failures; but the rare and outstanding success becomes the parent of great improvement. The prize winning steer at the Livestock Show usually is the result of breeding for increased variation, in which manner a winner is more likely to be produced. Thus it is possible to speed up the process of change, compared with the "natural processes" and the "normal processes" of selection, but there is a correspondingly great danger in it.

PROGRESS

WE SPEAK GLIBLY of progress. This term can usually be used, in casual conversation, without challenge or without any need to analyze its meaning. Each person thinks of illustrations of what are, to him, instances of progress that give meaning to the term "progress."

This discussion of liberty is of such a nature, however, that it might be advisable to focus its meaning a little closer. What is progress?

Most everyone accepts a discovery in medicine, like the germ theory of disease and the development of vaccines, as illustrating progress. Not so clearly acceptable as progress is some discovery in a controversial area. Some persons, for instance, hold the faith that if God had intended man to fly, He would have provided him with natural wings; they do not accept the development of the airplane as being progress. Some persons do not accept the automobile as being progress, for various reasons. And some even question whether a medical discovery is progress.

In Appendix I has been given certain concepts essential to this discussion of what is and what is not progress. The faiths defined therein are pertinent to these conclusions.

The first step is to concede that the right of judgment as to what is progress rests with each individual. No one person is deemed qualified to pass judgment for all of us. No one person can, in fact, appraise the matter for any other person (Appendix I, #7).

It might seem from this that there would be no way to label anything as "progress," because of conflicting views and appraisals. What some accept as progress will be rejected by others, and differences of opinion precludes unanimity in every instance.

A further difficulty is due to the fact that these appraisals are subjective matters. It cannot be known with certainty what any one person thinks about whether or not something deserves the label of "progress." How, then, could an objective label of "progress" ever be attached to anything?

Despite all these difficulties, it seems possible to speak of progress with an important meaning relevant to this discussion of liberty and its effects on progress.

The first step is to recognize that a person's acts under liberty offer some objective evidence about his subjective motivations, in the same manner as a mirror or periscope may be used to reflect an object which is not accessible to direct view. Whereas this type of reflection is not of the nature of certain proof, it serves as a basis for useful evidence where nothing better is available.

The free market, in like manner, offers evidence as to what a consumer wants, even thought this too is purely subjective. It serves as a guide to producers — the only available guide, and one that works quite well, it seems. The entire business world, in a liberal economy, rests on this form of evidence as its guide to production.

If these judgments are to be depended upon, however, there must be liberty so that persons may freely express their subjective appraisals. Lacking liberty, reflections will become diluted with an unknown form and amount of misrepresentation. So the first requisite in judging the nature of progress is that there be liberty, so that individuals can express their appraisals freely. It may be assumed that under liberty persons will increasingly accept and approve what, in the universal order of things, may fairly be called progress. The importance of liberty in the test of progress is so close as to suggest that liberty is essentially the same as progress.

Acceptance of truth and an increase in the practices that are harmonious with truth will not, of course, be unanimous or instantaneous once a discovery has been made, for reasons discussed in Appendix I. But it must be assumed that there will be an increasing acceptance of truth under liberty, and so the test of progress is to be found in this degree of acceptance. That is why, based on the faiths expressed in Appendix I, it seems possible to speak of progress with meaning and for an important purpose, as follows:

Progress is any change in belief or in concept, or in their applications into "devices," which stands up under the tests of time and experience so as to have increasing acceptance among free people. In a word, it is an expression of truth or of applied truth, as tested by the only means at our disposal.

It is not necessary that there be unanimity of opinion before a thing can be termed progress. If it were, there could never be any "progress" at all. It is to be tested, instead, through a sort of continuous vote wherein each person's opinion is tested, and respected along with that of each other person. The "wisdom" of the egotist is given no more weight than that of any other person.

This concept of progress is one that allows dissenters. A single person may reject what others accept as progress, as his right under liberty. But he is not thereby empowered to cast a vote for another, either.

So when the discoverer peers into the unknown and finds something previously obscure — some new gadget, some new picture, some new symphony, some new idea or concept — the test of acceptance over time by a free people becomes the only available test of its worthiness and acceptibility in terms of human destiny and harmony with natural law and purpose. Thus a decisive change under liberty is what is meant herein by the term "progress."

LIMITATIONS OF THE MEASURE
OF LIBERTY

THE MEASURE OF LIBERTY given in Part Two of this book has deficiencies. It both overstates and understates the presumed correct figure, for various reasons and by unknown amounts.

Every error in the data on which this measure has been based carries over, of course, into the derived figure.

In all probability the net effect is to err on the low side, so that it understates the loss of liberty in the United States or in any other country where it might be applied. Some of the causes of error will be given so that other persons may make their own guesses as to what might be the figure after correction for these errors.

As has been discussed previously, this measure relates to economic liberty. This is not the only form of liberty and therefore this measure may either overstate or understate the loss of liberty as a whole, depending on the comparative degree of loss of liberty in other realms. But economic liberty pervades the entire problem and is an absolute requisite to liberty in general.

This measure of liberty is one that tests what happens to productive income, according to the concept in the national income from which it is derived. The presence or absence of liberty is, then, weighed according to each person's contribution to the production of goods and services as represented in the national income. Complete liberty in the spending of money that one may receive as a gift from the government, such as relief grants, is not allowed to affect the level of liberty according to this measure; the test of liberty is made at the point of its payment for something having been produced, and it is a question of whether or not the person who produced the income was allowed liberty in its use. Any other course would result in a test of liberty that would class one as fully free if he had liberty in the use of money received as a result of violated liberty. A dollar of income, once enslaved, was treated as a slavery dollar from there on.

FOR LIBERTY TO BE at a maximum there must be some government, or otherwise have the same functions performed by some other means. Whatever the amount of its necessary costs, that amount should not be considered as a violation of liberalism in society.

How much of the 29 cent part of the dollar, taken for governmental costs in the United States in 1947, would be allowable under liberalism? That question must remain unanswered until much more work has been done to analyze liberty in relation to the many activities of present-day government. Certain functions of government are invaluable to liberty, but these should not be highly expensive to operate; a Supreme Court, for instance, is not very costly and is a small part of the budget of a nation these days. A guess is that only a small part of the 29 cents, perhaps even less than 5 cents of it, would qualify under liberalism, if we ignore the costs of existing contracts which originated in illiberal acts.

Everything which government does in excess of this proper sphere involves a loss of liberty. All this excess drains from the citizen some of the product of their labor — "the sweat of the brow of the working man" — by force or by threat of force. It may be used to finance the costs of further loss of liberty, having a double effect in the destruction of liberty because of both the taking and its use. It may be used to operate governmental monopoly, so that citizens are not allowed to compete on an equal basis. But the fact remains that, with few or no exceptions, the excess taken by government represents a loss of liberty to the citizens of the country.

The excess that the government takes is no longer available for the citizen to spend as he wishes, as required under liberty. It may be said that the people want these services and would buy them anyhow if they were performed by private business instead of by government. But the slave who is given some turnips by his master cannot be called free economically because of the fact that he might have wanted to buy some turnips with some of his wages as a free man, had he been free. The citizen, likewise, is not judged to be free because of the fact that he might have bought, in a free market, services similar to those offered by the governmental monopoly where users and non-users alike are forced to pay the costs in their tax bills.

Acquiescence of the citizens to that part of their taxes in excess of what is necessary to preserve liberty is no evidence that liberty has not been lost thereby. Loss of liberty is not to be measured by the extent of refusal to pay taxes any more than slavery is to be measured by the degree of rebellion of the slaves. Slaves are none the less slaves because they are not always attached to their masters by a chain!

THE LOSSES OF LIBERTY not included in the measure herein explained probably exceed the overstatements.

A prisoner who is allowed 20 cents a day for working in the prison laundry, and who is free to spend all his income as he likes for candy or cigarettes, can hardly be called economically free. He might be able to earn $8 a day if he were free to compete in the economic world outside the prison walls.

A full measure of liberty, if it were available, would also take into account the income that is lost because of a lack of liberty. The income thus lost should be included with that part of a person's income that is taken away from him by force, in measuring the loss of economic liberty. In one part he is unfree because the income has been taken away from him in violation of liberty, whereas in the other part he is unfree, without liberty, because he never received the income in the first place; there is no difference between the two, so far as a measure of lost liberty is concerned.

The lost opportunities for additional income may result from the monopolies of government. A person is liable, for instance, to a fine of $500 or six months in jail for competing with the government and carrying a message for hire if it comes under the government's definition of first class mail.

Lost opportunities for income may result from monopolies of private business. Or they may result from the activities of certain trade organizations, or labor unions, or by some other agencies or persons. All of these, however, are possible only because the government fails to perform its proper function of preserving a climate wherein liberty can prevail and where full opportunity exists for the citizens under economic liberty, as previously defined.

Restrictions on free competition include all monopolies and all restrictions of free internal and international trade. All of these violate economic liberty by reducing income.

The administrative costs of handling a certain control operated by the government greatly understates the total loss of liberty which it entails, in most instances. The cost aspect is like that of a slaveholder who may spend no more than the equivalent of one-tenth of what the slave produces as the cost of hiring an overseer to hold the slaves under the yoke of complete slavery; it is not necessary to spend all that the slave produces as the cost of depriving him of his liberty.

The calculated cost of government includes nothing for the free radio time that is allowed to one or another branch of government, used to "explain" something and to advocate that which it advocates. The cost this free time, even at the lowest commercial rates charged to a private citizen, would total to a fantastic amount each year. Not alone that, but the viewpoints of governmental officials are given audience without charge; counter viewpoints, which the citizens may hold, can be aired only by paying the high costs of radio time in most instances.

Stalin has been able to maintain the Russian people in near-complete economic slavery by the use of far less than all of their incomes. We have noted that only 29 cents out of each dollar of income produced was being taken by the Russian government in 1929-1930, yet this amount was sufficient to administer and maintain almost complete slavery of the Russian people.

Is it not possible for a government at a very small cost to enact all the legislation necessary to illegalize essentially all economic liberty? Over-all wage and price controls would do it — even "standby controls," which is like a standby overseer of a group of prisoners or slaves. The costs of administering and enforcing these edicts, when added to the costs of enacting the laws, far understates the loss of liberty that is involved. All that is necessary is to frighten the subjects into submission, by the cheapest and most "efficient" means available. A horse thoroughly broken to harness seldom feels the whip.

INDEX